Celebrating Muḥammad

STUDIES IN
COMPARATIVE RELIGION

Frederick M. Denny, General Editor

CELEBRATING MUḤAMMAD

Images of the Prophet in Popular Muslim Poetry

by

Ali S. Asani
Kamal Abdel-Malek

in collaboration with
Annemarie Schimmel

UNIVERSITY OF SOUTH CAROLINA PRESS

Published in Columbia, South Carolina by the
University of South Carolina Press

Manufactured in the United States of America

99 98 97 96 95 5 4 3 2 1

Library of Congress Cataloging-in-Publication Data

Asani, Ali Sultaan Ali.
Celebrating Muḥammad : images of the prophet in popular Muslim poetry / by Ali S. Asani, Kamal Abdel-Malek, in collaboration with Annemarie Schimmel.
p. cm.
Includes bibliographical references (p.) and index.
ISBN 1–57003–050–2
1. Muḥammad, Prophet, d. 632—In literature. 2. Islamic poetry—History and criticism. 3. Muḥammad, Prophet, d. 632—Cult. I. Abdel-Malek, Kamal. II. Schimmel, Annemarie. III. Title.
PJ814.M83A84 1995
809′.93351—dc20 95–10341

REMEMBRANCE

Sultaan Ali Asani
1929–1994

O soul at peace return to your Lord.
—Qur'ān *Sūra* 89:27

This book is warmly dedicated to Charles J. Adams.

CONTENTS

General Editor's Preface ix
Preface xi
Note on Transliteration xv
Prologue 1
Introduction 10
Part 1: The Prophet Muḥammad in Indo-Muslim Poetry
1. Background and Introduction 19
2. The Bridegroom Prophet 29
3. The Rain Cloud and the Prophet 37
Part 2: The Prophet Muḥammad in an Egyptian Narrative Ballad
4. Introduction 49
5. The Text 54
6. Text Analysis 60
7. The Texture 70
Epilogue 75
Appendix 1: Selection of Poetry in Praise of the Prophet 81
Appendix 2: A Note on Poetic Genres 107
Select Bibliography 110
Index of Terms 115
Index of Proper Names 118
Index of Quranic References 126

GENERAL EDITOR'S PREFACE

Among the world religions, Islam is arguably the least understood and the one most often viewed in a negative light by outsiders. Moreover, among history's greatest religious personalities, the Arabian prophet Muḥammad has evoked the most contrary perceptions and responses. These range from viciously negative caricatures and distortions by medieval Christians to outright veneration from Muslims, who view their Prophet as the model of what it means to be a complete human being. Happily, recent decades have seen Muḥammad emerging in Western views in a way more reflective of his spiritual and moral greatness. But even so, biographical treatments have emphasized Muḥammad's historical career more than what he as an enduring religious figure means for Muslims in all periods.

There is, as the authors of this sensitive appreciation make abundantly clear, a difference between the Muḥammad of history and the Prophet of faith, to adapt a formula that has been applied to Jesus, who was a historical religious reformer in ancient Palestine, on one hand, and on the other the Christ who is always contemporary for the believing community. If the emphasis on Jesus has usually been on his supernatural, indeed divine, nature as the Incarnation of God, then the emphasis on Muḥammad—at least for outsiders, even when respectful—has focused more on the Prophet's political, social, military, and judicial achievements and functions than on his profound spirituality. But it is Muḥammad's spirituality that is key for Muslim consciousness and that provided the authority and meaning for the momentous historical events in the founding of the Muslim community.

Although it is grossly incorrect to refer to the religion of Islam as "Muhammadanism," it is nevertheless true that the Muslim community, the *umma*, is very much an empowered fellowship that continues to cultivate and hand down the Prophet's charisma through memory, practices, and institutions. Some of the agents and transmitters of Muḥammad's *sunna,* his "custom," are formal and even legal, while others are spontaneous and creative. This book treats the latter mode in its focus on vernacular poetry in praise of Muḥammad. The authors have provided interpretations of how the Prophet has been and continues to be viewed by Muslim devotees through poetic celebrations of key events in his biography, events which take flight as hagiography at many points.

There are very few studies such as the present one in the history of scholarship on Muḥammad, studies that focus not on the external Muḥammad as known in standard histories but on what the Norwegian historian of religions Tor Andrae, in his epochal study called *The* **Person** *of Muhammad in the Teaching and Faith of His Community (Die Person Muhammeds in Lehre und Glauben seiner Gemeinde* [Stockholm, 1918]; my emphasis). Annemarie Schimmel, one of the leading Western scholars of Islam of the century, whose own work has done so much to advance our knowledge and understanding of the Muḥammad of faith, provides the introduction for this book and has collaborated in the writing of the epilogue, as well. Her colleagues Ali Asani and Kamal Abdel-Malek, for their part, transport us to the special, beautiful worlds of Sindhi, Urdu, and colloquial Arabic verse composed under the spell of Muḥammad's abiding presence in the Muslim community's soul. The result is a volume that offers a generous comparative view of a variety of pious discourses within the diversely complex Muslim community, while it invites us to reflect comparatively on how other religious communities celebrate, cultivate, and preserve for posterity the teaching and example of their founders.

Frederick Mathewson Denny

PREFACE

In this book we will explore various portrayals of the prophet Muḥammad in a number of popular poetic traditions from the Islamic world. We have drawn on material—most of which is examined here for the first time—from Egyptian Arabic, Sindhi, Urdu, and Turkish sources, rendered in a variety of literary forms ranging from the classical ode to the popular ballad. Our book is, in effect, a study of Islam in local contexts with the veneration of the prophet Muḥammad as its unifying theme. We have consciously avoided the conventional dichotomization between elite and popular Islam or great and little or high and low traditions. We do not deny the existence of these forms of Islamic interpretation and practice; rather, we regard Islam as one integral tradition where the so-called folk and elite do meet and integrate more often than is usually assumed.

Not surprisingly, marriage as a means of uniting two unrelated entities is the prevailing motif in our study. The prophet Muḥammad is literally portrayed as the bridegroom in the Egyptian narrative ballad where he is wedded to Khadīja, and metaphorically in Sindhi poems where the poet's bride-soul longs for union with the Prophet-groom.

The book's prologue acquaints readers, especially those not familiar with Islam, with basic ideas of God and prophecy in the religion as well as the significant role played by the prophet Muḥammad in Islamic piety. The prologue particularly highlights the different ways in which Muslims relate to their beloved Prophet. The introduction, written by Annemarie Schimmel, examines the range and depth of Muslim veneration of the prophet Muḥammad as it is generally expressed in Islamic religious and mystical poetry. It draws on examples from regions as varied as Turkey, Iran, and South Asia. Part 1, then, leads us into the Islamic tradition of the Indian subcontinent and analyzes the veneration of the Prophet in the works of two prominent Indo-Muslim poets who represent different aspects of the tradition. The first, ʿAbd ur-Raʾūf Bhaṭṭī (d. 1752), whose work was heavily influenced by the rural folk traditions of the Sind region in the Lower Indus Valley, ranks among the earliest poets to compose poems in praise of the prophet Muḥammad in Sindhi; the second, Muḥsin Kākorawī (d. 1905), the Prophet's great Urdu panegyrist, belonged to the highly literate urban culture of Islamic Northern India. Both poets dress the person of their beloved Prophet in their native linguistic and poetic attire—now as a bridegroom, now as a rain cloud of mercy.

In part 2 we travel to the Middle East, specifically the ancient country of Egypt. These chapters examine the portrayal of the Prophet in Egyptian popular poetry—popular in the sense that it includes orally transmitted poems of unknown authorship as well as colloquial compositions by literate and known authors. Among various types of popular eulogies in honor of the Prophet, part 2 focuses on a narrative ballad in colloquial Egyptian Arabic (CEA). The ballad tells the story of Muḥammad's trading journey to Syria and his marriage to his beloved wife, Khadīja. This section then analyzes the folk themes, imagery, and diction of the ballad and discusses the differences between them and the classical accounts of these events as found in the oldest biography of Ibn Isḥāq (d. ca. 767). The intent here is to demonstrate the powerful influence of local Egyptian oral traditions and hagiography in the depiction of the Prophet's life.

Following is an epilogue (written in collaboration with Annemarie Schimmel) and two appendixes. The first appendix contains selected poems translated from Sindhi and Urdu (by Ali Asani) and colloquial Egyptian Arabic (by Kamal Abdel-Malek). The translations from Sindhi, which appear in *Religions of India in Practice,* ed. Donald Lopez (Princeton, forthcoming 1995), are reproduced here with the kind permission of Princeton University Press. The second appendix describes some of the more popular literary forms employed in the Islamic world for composing poetry in praise of Muḥammad. Unless otherwise noted, all translations in the text are by the authors.

We would like to acknowledge our debt to Professor Annemarie Schimmel for her very valuable comments on our portions of the book and for her constant encouragement and genuine care. She has devoted many years to studying the veneration of the Prophet in various Islamic literatures and we are honored by her collaboration. We would also like to express our gratitude to the many friends and colleagues who have supported our work but whom we cannot mention here individually because of space constraints. In particular, we would like to mention the following people: Professor Charles Adams for having suggested important changes to an earlier draft of part 2, and Pierre

Cachia, Issa Boullata, Donald Little, Susan Slymovics, William Graham, Zoe Hersov, and Dwight Reynolds for their comments on various parts of the manuscript. We would especially like to thank Michael Currier for having devoted time and effort in reading several drafts and for his editorial comments. Rachel Rockenmacher of Harvard's Department of Near Eastern Languages and Civilizations diligently prepared the manuscript for final editing. We are grateful to Professor Frederick Denny for having suggested the idea of writing this book and for his encouragement and understanding whenever we approached him with our many requests. Special thanks are due to Markaz al-Funūn ash-Shaʿbiyya (Center for Folk Arts) in Cairo and its director, Mr. Ḥusnī Luṭfī, for having provided valuable recordings of Egyptian folk ballads and eulogies in honor of the prophet Muḥammad. Lastly, and respectfully, we are indebted to our families, especially Shirin (Ali's mother) and Diane Tompkins (Kamal's wife), all of whom have selflessly supported each of us individually and have deservingly earned our gratitude.

Ali Asani
Kamal Abdel-Malek

NOTE ON TRANSLITERATION

The system of transliteration for Arabic in this book follows the one used by the Institute of Islamic Studies, McGill University, with two exceptions: *tāʾ marbūt̤a* is transliterated as "a," not "ah," except in the *iḍāfa* where it is rendered as "at"; the Arabic letter ط is transliterated as "t̤" to distinguish it from the Urdu/Sindhi ٹ and ٽ which are represented as "ṭ." The spoken Arabic vocables are transliterated according to the way they are pronounced in colloquial Egyptian (e.g., *yawm al-qiyāma, mujtahid, al-nabī* become, respectively, *yom il-ʾiyāma, mugtahid, in-nabī*). The helping "i" vowel, used in Egyptian Arabic to break the inadmissible sequence of three consonants (as in *min baᶜd madḥ an-nabī*) is represented as a short vowel connected to the vocable with a dash: *min baᶜd-i madḥ-i n-nabī.*

For Indo-Persian and Indo-Muslim vernaculars, the book follows the transliteration system of J. Platts as employed in *A Dictionary of Urdu, Classical Hindi, and English* (Oxford University Press, 1960).

CELEBRATING MUḤAMMAD

Prologue

This is a book about Muḥammad, the Prophet of Islam, who was one of the most influential figures in human history. So powerful and radiant was his personality that almost fourteen hundred years after his death he remains a significant focus of love and devotion for millions of Muslims all over the world. As Constance Padwick has observed, no one can estimate the power of Islam as a religion without first taking into account that at the heart of the tradition is love for the prophet Muḥammad.[1] She describes this love as a warm human emotion which the simplest peasant can share with the most sophisticated intellectual or mystic. This study is a celebration of this love, portraying some of the ways it is manifested in popular Muslim literature from culturally diverse regions of the Islamic world.

There have been few studies that have explored the intensity and depth of veneration that Muslims feel towards their beloved Prophet. Not many books on Islam attempt to explore the significance of millions of Muslims every day reciting the *ṣalawāt*—a formula invoking blessing on the prophet Muḥammad whom they affectionately call *ḥabīb Allāh* (God's beloved). Indeed, the subject of Islamic piety and devotion in general, especially at a popular level, is not well understood and its true nature not well appreciated. Perhaps the fact that the faith of Islam is associated in the popular media with violence, terrorism, political militancy, and other negative images has contributed a great deal to the sad neglect of Islamic devotional life. While this is not the place to discuss the nature and origins of these misconceptions, it is sufficient to say that sometimes even reasonably educated non-Muslims are highly surprised to learn that the central message of Islam, like that of Christianity and Judaism, is monotheism:

1. *Muslim Devotions* (London: SPCK, 1960), 145.

God is one; "He has not begotten nor is He begotten," as chapter 112 of the Qurʾān states. The Islamic profession of faith begins with the sentence "There is no deity save God (Allāh)," a statement that Jews and Christians would readily embrace. Muslims have developed a vast theological literature around this central idea, and the goal of every Muslim interpreter has been to prove by theological, philological, philosophical, or mystical exegesis that there is only one God, whom the Qurʾān surrounds with the ninety-nine Most Beautiful Names. There is no sin worse in Islam than associating anything as an equal with God, who is creator, sustainer, and judge on the day of judgment. Indeed, as is well known, the word *islām* (belonging to the same verbal root in Arabic as the word *salām*, or "peace") means "submission to the will of the one God" who knows best what is good for His creation. Hence one who submits to God is called a *Muslim* (feminine *Muslima*), literally "a submitter."

Perhaps some of the greatest misconceptions about the Islamic faith concern Muḥammad, its prophet. In medieval Europe, for example, a whole range of negative judgments were passed upon this man whom Muslims venerate. Muḥammad was variously depicted as an idol worshipper, an arch-schismatic, an epileptic, a kind of antichrist, heretic, and even as a cardinal who, having been thwarted in his ambitions to become pope, founded his own religion. Usually called Mahomet (the Scottish mispronunciation *Mahound* led the Prophet's name to be translated as "devil" or "spirit of darkness"), he was viewed by non-Muslims as a kind of a supreme god that his followers adored like a golden idol. The figure of Muḥammad aroused so much fear and hatred that Dante, in the *Divine Comedy*, saw nothing wrong in condemning this man who has so positively influenced the lives of millions to the deepest abyss of Hell. Frequently in polemic literature Muḥammad was criticised for his involvement in politics and warfare and even more for his "excessive sexuality." After the death (in 619) of his first wife, the faithful Khadīja (who unswervingly supported him from the day the divine revelations overcame him), Muḥammad married a number of women, mainly widows or divorced women. For critics this was proof of his questionable and licentious character. The fact that marriage was his *sunna* (his way of life) contradicted the religious ideals of medieval Christian Europe, with its strong emphasis on celibacy and virginity.

From a Muslim point of view, the failure of non-Muslims to understand the role of Muḥammad has been, and still is, one of the greatest obstacles to an appreciation of Islam as understood from within. For Muslims, Muḥammad (born in the Arabian city of Mecca in or about 570) was sent by God as "a bringer of good tidings" and as "a warner."

He is seen as "a shining lamp" for those that err in the darkness of infidelity, and as "mercy for the worlds" to teach the law that God has given humanity so that it might be saved from the horrors of eternal damnation. Muḥammad taught obedience and worship of the one Lord, maintaining that these are the duties of every believer. He also taught that whatever exists was created to praise the Creator in its own silent eloquence. Muḥammad was the one to whom God's will was revealed and who was called to bring to his followers the same divine message as had been given to previous people; for God has never left His creatures without guidance. Islam therefore recognizes and respects the earlier prophets, beginning with Adam. Among them, Moses and Jesus are given pride of place—Jesus, in Muslim tradition, is the prophet preceding Muḥammad and born by the Virgin Mary through the inbreathing of God's spirit. However, he is not believed to be God's son and was not, according to the Qurʾān, crucified, but taken into heaven. Besides the twenty-eight prophets mentioned by name in the Qurʾān, the Muslim can acknowledge others as well, provided these prophets have appeared before Muḥammad, who is the seal of prophets—that is, the one who brought the final, definitive revelation, the Qurʾān (Recitation) in the Arabic language.

The Qurʾān, the scripture of Islam, revealed by God to Muḥammad between 610 and 632 and later arranged into 114 chapters (*sūras*), forms the fundamental core of the faith. For a Muslim, listening to the Qurʾān means listening to the Divine voice—even though most Muslims, being non-Arabs, do not understand the words and depend on translations and commentaries by religious scholars for their comprehension of its contents. It is a book with an inimitable style, possessing divine beauty and power. The beautiful recitation of the Qurʾān is therefore a most edifying and sublime act, and the art of calligraphy, the typical Islamic art form, grew out of the wish to write the word of God as perfectly as possible. Though the sacred book has been translated into many languages (including Latin as early as 1143), for the Muslim, a translation of the Qurʾān is strictly impossible. Because the Qurʾān is considered to be God's own word, its different levels of understanding can never be offered in a language other than the original Arabic. At best a translation is only an explanation of the book's meaning: one interpretation among others.

Islamic belief concerning the divine origin of the Qurʾān has meant that Muslims have never considered Muḥammad to be its author—he was merely its transmitter. As a Swahili Muslim preacher in East Africa explained to his congregation recently, the Prophet's role was somewhat like that of a transistor radio. Although this transistor metaphor may be too simplistic,[2] it illustrates the orthodox Muslim position. The Qurʾān emphasizes Muḥammad's humanity by calling him "a human being like you to whom the revelation was brought."[3] For the Muslim, the similarities between the Qurʾān and Judaeo-Christian religious texts, including the Old Testament, is not problematic: God's revelation to humanity is basically one, and the different scriptures are simply earthly manifestations from a single source—God's heavenly book. The divine word was poured into the Prophet, who was the pure vessel of divine grace. In the Qurʾān, he is called *ummī,* an Arabic term that originally meant "one sent to the *umma,*" the "gentiles," or those who have not yet been blessed by a revelation. However, this word quickly assumed the meaning of illiterate, because Muḥammad had to be immaculate in order to receive the divine word, which was to be "inlibrated"[4] in the Qurʾān—just as in Christianity Mary had to be a virgin to give birth to Jesus, the divine word incarnate. This revelation corrects parts of the previous sacred scriptures (Torah, Psalms, and Gospels) which, the Qurʾān claims, have been partly altered by Jews and Christians, according to their sectarian biases.

Ironically, the most important factor contributing to the lack of understanding about Muḥammad and his relationship to his followers may in fact lie in the traditional academic approach to this subject. For the most part (with the exception of Tor Andrae's *Die Person Muhammeds in Lehre und Glauben seiner Gemeinde* and Annemarie Schimmel's works *And Muhammad Is His Messenger* and *Und Muhammad ist Sein Prophet*) scholarship on the Prophet has been characterized by an overwhelming emphasis on his historical personality. There have been innumerable biographies focusing on his life (birth, career, death); types of influences on his thought; motives for his sociopolitical activity; the development of his consciousness; and on his accomplishments. Several works have striven to offer the results of painstaking research into the question of Muḥammad's "borrowing," wittingly or

2. Some Muslims, mindful of the complexities of divine revelation *(waḥy),* have argued that Muḥammad's heart and mind did play some role in this process. Fazlur Rahman, for example, citing Qurʾānic passages that tell that the revelation was brought down on the heart of Muḥammad, rejects the simplistic notion that God's message was communicated through Muḥammad in a mechanical manner. See Frederick Mathewson Denny, "Fazlur Rahman: Muslim Intellectual," *Muslim World* 79, no. 2 (1989): 98–100.

3. *Sūra* 41:6.

4. Henry Austryn Wolfson, *The Philosophy of the Kalam* (Cambridge, London: Harvard University Press, 1976), 246.

unwittingly, stories from the Old Testament and sectarian Christian texts and their incorporation into "his" Qur'ān. No doubt, these biographical studies by European scholars, especially the more recent ones, have been much more objective than the works of earlier generations and do better justice in treating the Prophet's personality. Yet, we would argue that to truly understand the significance of the Prophet to Muslims, it would be more appropriate and more fruitful for us to probe the figure of Muḥammad as the paradigm, or model, for Muslim life. The exemplar, the guide, the intercessor, the kind and loyal friend, the beloved—these are some of the roles that Muslims have seen in their Prophet. In other words, our questions should not center exclusively upon the historical Muḥammad of seventh-century Arabia, but the Muḥammad of faith. A scholarly study of Islam should be concerned then with the role Muḥammad has played in the lives of Muslims through the centuries as the messenger of God. Such an approach, in fact, resembles in many ways that taken by Jaroslav Pelikan in his study of Jesus through the centuries.[5]

Perhaps the best way to appreciate the role of Muḥammad in Islamic piety is to explore the significance of the second part of the Islamic profession of faith: "Muḥammad is God's messenger." At one level, this simple sentence establishes Islam as a distinct religious system. While most monotheists can agree with the statement that there is only one God, belief in Muḥammad as God's messenger and Prophet defines Islamic identity—for it distinguishes Muslims from peoples of other faiths. At another level, the acknowledgement of Muḥammad as God's messenger *par excellence* defines the practical and legal aspects of Islam. Whoever takes this statement seriously is bound to obey the law which was revealed to Muḥammad: he/she has to perform the daily prayers; pay the alms tax; keep the fast during the month of Ramadan; and perform once in his/her life the pilgrimage to Mecca. If he/she does not practice all these duties then he/she has at least to admit that these are duties of the believer.

On issues that the Qur'ān did not regulate or was unclear on, the custom or way (*sunna*) of the Prophet was called upon as the standard or measure of the norms of religious life. From the earliest periods of Islamic history, the Prophet's words and actions were related time and again by his family and those close to him, and these reports (the *ḥadīth*) were often used to explain certain remarks in the Qur'ān which

5. Jaroslav Jan Pelikan, *Jesus Through the Centuries: His Place in the History of Culture* (New Haven: Yale University Press, 1985).

were short and enigmatic; thus, the *ḥadīth* developed into a kind of early commentary on the Qurʾān. It is understandable that the number of stories about Muḥammad grew in proportion after the Prophet's death. Everyone knows how easy it is to surround a beloved person or a role model with all kinds of wonderful stories and ascribe words of wisdom to him or her which may reflect the person's intentions but which were never really spoken by the deceased. Small wonder, then, that the sayings and tales about the Prophet increased from decade to decade. In the ninth century several Muslim scholars produced collections of those *ḥadīth* which, according to all rules of criticism, were truthful and correct. Their collections remained a guide for the community through the centuries. The traditional way is to strive for a perfect *imitatio Muḥammadi*—following the Prophet's example in every detail of daily life including even matters of personal hygiene and dress. Recently one observes a tendency to interpret the *ḥadīth* literature not so much according to its literal meaning (as in, Muḥammad used to wind his turban in this or that way) but rather to ponder the way in which Muslims of the first generation might have understood the intended meaning of a certain saying or order. For the legalistically minded Muslims, the Prophet has become the lawgiver *par excellence*. For them, imitation of Muḥammad and his custom establishes legal, personal, and pietistic norms for the faithful.

The development of theological and mystical doctrines concerning Muḥammad's person contributed other significant dimensions to his role in Islamic religious life. Muḥammad never claimed special honors for himself, even though the Qurʾān asserts that God and the angels bless him. Consequently, the blessing for the Prophet (*ṣalawāt*) developed into one of the most important formulas in Muslim life: according to popular belief, to bless the Prophet brings innumerable recompenses in this world and the next. Yet, Muḥammad felt that he was only a "slave to whom revelation was granted," and the designation *ʿabduhu* (His slave, meaning God's slave) was regarded as his highest epithet. It pointed to the mysterious night journey alluded to at the beginning of the Qurʾānic *Sūra* 17: "Praised be He who traveled at night with His servant" and to the parallel visionary experience related in *Sūra* 53, where again the term "His slave" is used. These allusions to the Prophet's spiritual experiences, especially during his celestial journey (*miʿrāj*), gave rise to voluminous literature in Islamic mystical circles concerning his true spiritual status. Muḥammad's *miʿrāj* formed for the mystics of Islam the prototype of the ascent of their own souls to higher spiritual realms. He became for them not only the beloved of God but, even more, a luminous being who did not cast a shadow.

Some went so far as to say that he was created, as a white pearl or a column of crystal, from the divine light prior to the creation of Adam. Such speculation led to the formulation of concepts such as the preeternal "Light of Muḥammad" (*nūr Muḥammad*) and the "Muḥammad reality" (*ḥaqīqa Muḥammadiyya*). In the course of time, among such mystically minded circles, Muḥammad reached the status of the perfect man (*al-insān al-kāmil*) and was considered the beginning and end of creation. This concept became popular through the extra-Qurʾānic saying attributed to God: *laulāka mā khalaqtu'l aflāka* (If you had not been (i.e., but for your sake) I would not have created the spheres). For many Muslims, some of these ideas bordered on heresy.

Both friends and followers also told stories of Muḥammad's miracles. Some of these are alluded to in the Qurʾān; other stories pertain to events during his life. According to the most popular of these, Muḥammad is said to have split the moon. This miracle is elaborated from a verse in the Qurʾānic *Sūra* 54: "The hour drew near and the moon was split." From such stories developed a rich hagiographic tradition which endows the Prophet with supernatural gifts and almost superhuman powers. The tradition also shows him as extremely gentle and kind, caring for the poor and the needy but also for animals. His kindness culminates in his role as intercessor on doomsday when he will request God not to let anyone among his community remain eternally in Hell. Generations of believers have pinned their hope on this role of the Prophet who will arrive with his green flag of praise to lead the community to paradise. Indeed, the role of Muḥammad as intercessor is truly the most significant leitmotif of Prophet-oriented piety. The notion that a penitent sinner can be saved by Muḥammad's intercession and God's mercy led to all kinds of Muslims (ranging from learned scholars and ecstatic mystics, to popular minstrels and cunning statesmen) uttering countless prayers and verses, imploring the Prophet's intercession.

Muslims see their Prophet through a variety of lenses, and the role he plays in their lives differs according to the perspective they choose to adopt. Portrayals of Muḥammad in popular literature are strongly influenced by diverse interpretations of his status as well as local cultural and literary idioms. A village woman in Bangladesh may well conceive of her relationship to Muḥammad in an entirely different way than a Bedouin nomad in Saudi Arabia, or a peasant farmer in Pakistan. Frequently, Muslims disagree among themselves about the validity or appropriateness of certain ways of relating to Muḥammad or portraying him.

Typically, more conservative Muslims are concerned that excessive veneration of the Prophet, by compromising strict monotheism, leads to the gravest sin a Muslim could commit, *shirk* (associating or ascribing partners to God). These conservatives have also felt that this emotional and romantic piety contains too many foreign or non-Islamic elements of imagination and mythology to be compatible with basic Islamic conceptions of the divine and the institution of prophethood. They have probably been afraid that such legends and mystical flights of imagination might give the prophet Muḥammad a status similar to that of Jesus in Christianity. For example, in the fifteenth and sixteenth centuries the use of candles during the *maulūd* (the Prophet's birthday celebration) aroused fear among religious authorities that Christian, or infidel, influences were distorting the real role of the Prophet as delineated in the Qurʾān.[6] In this regard, we must mention the centuries-old controversy among Muslim theologians over the appropriateness of celebrating the Prophet's birthday, especially after it became a popular holiday in many parts of the Islamic world.[7] Although this festival is not explicitly sanctioned by the Qurʾān, more liberal schools of Islamic jurisprudence have permitted it as a praiseworthy innovation (*bidʿa*). In contrast, religious scholars of the strictly conservative Hanbali school have prohibited the event, for they feel that it elevates the Prophet to a divine-like status and makes him the object of inappropriate veneration. Thus, festivities marking Muḥammad's birthday are organized in almost every country of the contemporary Islamic world, with the exception of his birthplace in the Hanbali-influenced kingdom of Saudi Arabia.

Notwithstanding the reservations and objections that divide Muslims on the issue of prophetic veneration, the Prophet has remained the model and guide for all Islam. When God himself endorses Muḥammad's paradigmatic role in the Qurʾān by refering to him as *uswa ḥasana* (a beautiful model) (*Sūra* 33:21), does it not behoove the sincere believer to accept this divine sanction? Beyond this, the Prophet has become someone to whom one can entrust oneself—just as one entrusts oneself to a beloved and venerated member of the family. The constant presence of the Prophet as the kind and beloved, deeply venerated friend in Muslim society is a feeling of which most non-Muslims

6. Annemarie Schimmel, *And Muhammad Is His Messenger* (Chapel Hill: University of North Carolina Press, 1985), 146.

7. For a discussion of the early history and development of the festival and an analysis of some legal opinions concerning its legitimacy, see N. J. G. Kaptein, *Muhammad's Birthday Festival* (Leiden: E. J. Brill, 1993).

are not aware. It is this feeling of a close personal relationship that permeates the Islamic devotional poetry we analyze in this book.

The poetic traditions we examine here originate from several cultural regions that have played significant roles in the history of Islamic civilization. On account of differences inherent in the very nature of these traditions, we have had to employ differing methodologies in our analysis. Consequently, although the perspectives we offer in the book may vary, they are united in their focus on the depiction of the Prophet within local cultural and literary idioms. As noted in the preface, the book comprises three discussions—the introduction and two parts. We have arranged these discussions in a telescopic fashion, beginning in the introduction with a broad overview, or bird's-eye view, of major themes and symbols generally characteristic of devotional poetry in praise of the Prophet in most languages of the Islamic world. Part 1, on the devotional tradition in Islamic South Asia, is bifocal in its perspective for it examines—both in perspective and up close—poetry in praise of the Prophet in two Indic literatures (namely Sindhi and Urdu), highlighting the interactions of significant poetic symbols from different cultures. Part 2, on the Egyptian tradition, "zooms in" to provide a close-up of a single genre of popular literature in colloquial Egyptian Arabic. Through a detailed analysis of the popular account of the Prophet's marriage to Khadīja, the chapters in part 2 demonstrate the synthesis between folk and classical traditions in the ballad.

We hope the chapters that follow, notwithstanding the differences in their scope and outlook, provide a collage of images from which the reader can gain greater insight into the nature of Muslim devotion to the Prophet and learn what Muslim poets in the Arab and non-Arab world feel about him who has been described as "the best of humankind."

Introduction

by Annemarie Schimmel

The Rain of Grace
The Prophet Muḥammad in Islamic Devotional Poetry

Welcome, O friend of the poor and destitute
Welcome, O eternal soul, we welcome you.
Welcome, O cupbearer of the lovers, we welcome you.
Welcome, O darling of the Beloved,
Welcome, O much beloved of the Lord,
Welcome, O mercy for the worlds,
Welcome, O intercessor for the sinners
Only for you were Time and Space created.

These are lines from the *Mevlūd-i sharīf* by Suleyman Chelebi, a Turkish poet who died in 1419 in Bursa (the first capital of the Ottoman sultans). This *mevlūd* (or birth-poem) was my introduction to the veneration of the Prophet when my Turkish class read it during the fall of 1940 at the University of Berlin. I was fascinated by the beautiful way in which the poet, using a very simple meter and often an almost childish language, was able to convey to the reader or listener the feelings of a pious medieval Muslim who had long remembered the stories that were woven around the wondrous birth of Muḥammad. Stories from both learned and popular tradition, from very early days, describe all the miracles connected with the Prophet's birth, when his mother, Āmina, became aware of the radiant light that surrounded her. This light could even be observed in the castles of Bostra in Syria. The stories further describe her labor and the assistance of the Pharaoh's wife, as well as Mary, the mother of Jesus. During the night of the birth, all animals in the stables and the fields were telling each other that the luminous, final prophet had appeared as "Mercy for the worlds" (Qur'ān *Sūra* 21:107).

Many years later, I often had the opportunity of listening to the *mevlūd* in Turkish homes, and I always enjoyed both the words and the simple tune in which they were recited, interrupted by recitations from the Qurʾān and by prayers. It was a lovely experience, especially when artists participated in the musical part, as did Kani Karaca once in my house long before he became famous as the best reciter of religious music in Turkey.

But the part of the *mevlūd* recital I liked best was the custom of the audience getting up and touching each other's backs when the singer recited Āmina's tale of her experience: she is offered some heavenly sherbet, and:

> Drinking it I was immersed in light
> And could not discern myself from light.
> Then a white swan came with soft grey wings
> And he touched my back with gentle strength,
> And the King of Faith was born this night,
> Earth and Heaven were submersed in light.

The tender movement of touching the backs of friends in imitation of the blessing and caressing movement of the heavenly bird showed clearly that for my Turkish friends the Prophet was not at all someone far and remote in time and space, but a living force who seemed very close to his followers. All the legends that had been woven around his personality notwithstanding, the Prophet appeared as a human being, only distinguished as the bearer of God's final revelation. Through the veils of centuries of hagiography, the faithful Muslim could perceive that Muḥammad was the living model for all humans and that his *sunna* (his way of speaking and behaving) was followed in the same way as one might follow the example of a highly venerated elder of the family. One could speak to him and pour out one's heart before him because one knew that it was he who would appear on the day of judgment to intercede for his followers. During that dreaded hour when everyone else, including the innocent Jesus, will call out: *nafsī nafsī* (I myself [hope for salvation]), Muḥammad alone will march forth and call: *ummatī ummatī* (my community, my community [should be saved]) and will intercede even for the greatest sinners of the Muslim community. Is that not reason enough for a Muslim to sing of Muḥammad's kindness and to tell him of one's sorrows and needs?

To be sure, the absolute source of power and mercy is the one God, but when one looks at Muslim poetical expressions of the faith, in the form of long *qaṣīdas* (hymns addressed to the Creator and Judge in

Arabic, Persian, Turkish, and Indo-Muslim languages) one has the impression that poets are often confused as how to praise God, the all-powerful, adequately. They may find a way to give homage to Him by enumerating His contradictory attributes, the names under which He revealed Himself in the Qur'ān—the first and the last, the inner and the outward, the one who bestows life and He who bestows death, He who raises and He who lowers and does whatever He deems necessary and useful. Poems describing His unfathomable depth by hinting at the mysterious manner in which His beauty (*jamāl*) and His majesty (*jalāl*) together form the fabric of life of the world are abundant in the Muslim world.

But it is in the poems written in honor of the Prophet that the poets have opened their hearts, have expressed their hope in his intercession, and have praised the one who appears like the great rain cloud that stretches over the world to quicken the dried-up, lifeless hearts. And like rain—often called mercy (*raḥmat*) by villagers in Muslim areas—he is sent as "mercy for the worlds." Poets describe him as the one from whom the rose was grown during a night journey when a mysterious winged creature (Burāq) carried him through different spheres into God's presence; the drops of perspiration that fell from his face onto the ground grew into roses which still carry in them Muḥammad's fragrance. Popular ballads elaborate the miracles which were soon ascribed to him although Muḥammad himself refused the idea that he had performed any miracles other than conveying the words of the Qur'ān. But many miracles ascribed to him grew out of expressions used in the Qur'ān, like the description of the night journey, derived from the short remark in the Qur'ān (*Sūra* 17:1), which was often combined with the visionary account of the beginning of *Sūra* 53—"The Star." The "splitting of the moon" (*Sūra* 54:1) was a favorite topic that was particularly dear to Indian authors. This might be attributed to a ruler of Konkan who was converted to Islam when he observed that the moon was split during the night. This miracle laid, as it were, the foundations of the Muslim community in Southern India. But more frequent are stories outside Qur'ānic statements. Poets from both the great traditions of the big cities (the royal seats of Iran or Egypt) and those of the villages of Anatolia or Sind vied with each other in embellishing the miracle of the weeping palm trunk. It is said that a piece of wood upon which the Prophet used to put his hand—until a proper *minbar* (pulpit) was erected—then began to sigh because it missed the touch of the master's hand. "Should not humans feel the same longing for the Prophet?" the poets asked. Other poets, especially in the rural areas, would tell, in ever new variants, how the Prophet once helped a gazelle that had been trapped, and now pined to feed her kids, by entering the snare and freeing her. All of the poets knew according to centuries-old tales that the trees bowed before him and that the wolf and lizard attested to his rank as God's messenger as much as doors and walls greeted him and the pebbles in his hand sang his praise. Some of the folk poets in Turkey or in Sind say that one is able to hear, in the humming of the bees, the words of blessing for the Prophet and his family (*ṣalawāt sharīfa*) since this ensures that the honey will be sweet. And like the honey, the human heart will become sweetened by the constant recitation of the *ṣalawāt sharīfa*. Such loving descriptions fill the pages of numberless books, and allusions to these stories percolated into wedding songs and lullabies so that the Muslim child grows up with the idea of the Prophet as a loving friend of humanity. It is also believed that pious people might see him in their dreams, and such dreams are always true because Satan cannot assume the Prophet's form. One feels that Muḥammad is still alive, for stories and poems often tell how he would extend his hand from his *Rauẓa* (his mausoleum in Medina) to those who came imploring help or vindication from him; that is particularly frequent in the case of the *sayyids* (his descendants). However, verses expressing the poets' deep longing for Medina became increasingly popular in the later Middle Ages. This relationship, despite the Prophet's spiritual greatness, is often a very personal one that can be understood from popular poems in different parts of the world which describe events like his marriage to Khadīja, the mother of the faithful.

Another aspect of Muslim mystical prophetology that permeated Islamic devotional poetry is Muḥammad's luminous nature which manifested itself during his birth (according to legend light had been shining on the forehead of Muḥammad's father before he married Āmina). Popular tradition also claims that the Prophet did not cast a shadow, and that he was beauty personified—for it was his light that shone through Joseph (Yūsuf), the paragon of beauty. All previous prophets show only aspects of Muḥammad who is the sum total of laudable qualities. In the terminology of Ibn al-ʿArabī and his followers, Muḥammad is the *insān kāmil* (perfect man) in whom the divine names in their fullness are reflected while everyone else is the locus of manifestation for only one, or at best, a few, of these names. He alone is *al-jāmiʿ* (the comprehensive one).

Persian poets like Sanāʾī (d. 1131) have skillfully interpreted the first words of Qurʾānic chapter 93, *wa aḍ-ḍuḥā* ("By the morning light") as pertaining to the radiant beauty of Muḥammad while the first word of chapter 92, "By the night," was interpreted as referring to Muḥammad's black hair.

It is the concept of this Muḥammadan light *(nūr muḥammadī)* that played a central role in later Ṣūfī speculation. This belief is that God created Muḥammad from His own light so that Muḥammad's spiritual essence, like a column of light, stood in front of the Lord performing the ritual prayer long before God created everything else from it. These ideas were developed by Ṣūfīs such as Sahl at-Tustarī as early as the late ninth century and were then expanded and embellished by theologians and poets. They must have been widely known in the Muslim lands, for the myth that this primordial light—something like a radiant white pearl—began to perspire and that the different parts of the animated world were created from this perspiration is found in both medieval Bengal and sixteenth-century Turkey. Not surprisingly, even the Islamic literatures of sub-Saharan Africa are permeated by allusions to the prophetic light. The eighteenth-century West African poetess Asma bint Shehu acclaims in the Hausa language that the light of Muḥammad outshines in its brilliance any other light.

As we have already seen in the prologue, many theologians objected to this emotional and romantic piety that seemed to contain too many elements of non-Islamic imagination and myths. One can well understand their position that these were incompatible with the strict monotheistic tenets of Islam. Despite these theological objections, however, the veneration of the Prophet seems to have had something that fulfilled a deep need among large segments of the Muslim population; otherwise, the existence of an enormous corpus of poetry, legends, grand hymns, and simple folk songs about the Prophet cannot be explained.

Perhaps the most succinct expression of the deep love for, and faith in, the Prophet can be found in the works of one of his greatest admirers in our century, Muḥammad Iqbāl (d. 1938), whose prophetology contains all the traditional elements that had developed during the past fourteen hundred years. However, Iqbāl also highlights the practical aspects of the Prophet, who has to act in accordance with God's will by implementing the Divine order to ameliorate the world which he has been given as a fief, to be returned to God. In his *Jāvīdnāme* (1932) (the Book of Eternity) which, like so many great epical poems in the Muslim world, is modeled according to the story of the Prophet's heavenly journey, Iqbāl has described Muḥammad as "being in time and yet ruling time," but has especially dwelt upon his rank as *ʿabduhu* (His, i.e. God's, slave). The station of *ʿabduhu* is, as early Ṣūfīs have claimed, the highest rank a human being can reach. The true slave of God is, at the same time, the truly free person.

"You can deny God, but you cannot deny the Prophet." With these words, Iqbāl intends that it is through the Prophet that Islam becomes articulated as a religious system, and it is through him that Divine wisdom is revealed to humankind while God remains forever hidden in His essence behind the veils of divine names and attributes. As the dispenser of God's wisdom Muḥammad beckons to the eternal truth, and is therefore worthy of the believers' reverence and love. Here Iqbāl alludes to a role played by the Prophet for which generations of Muslims have always remained grateful, namely, the Prophet's role in conveying the message of Islam to the world and teaching humankind the way to approach God. Hence it was only natural for Iqbāl, like other Muslim poets, to depict the Prophet as a guide and leader to the truth. Muḥammad is the caravan leader who guides the community of believers to the Kaʿba in Mecca. Even more importantly, the Prophet provides an example of the way in which a supranational community of Muslims can and should be built, overcoming the obstacles created by prejudice and hatred. In the final analysis the prophet Muḥammad remains, even centuries after his death, a powerful force fostering unity within a culturally diverse Muslim community. All this has been expressed, in all the languages of the Muslim world, in poetry—the true reflection of the feelings of millions of believers.

PART 1

THE PROPHET MUḤAMMAD IN INDO-MUSLIM POETRY

CHAPTER 1

Background and Introduction

According to a legend prevailing in the Malabar region of India, a local Indian ruler (Shakarwatī Farmāḍ) had already converted to Islam within the lifetime of the prophet Muḥammad. The king, the legend tells us, became a Muslim after he witnessed the miracle of the splitting of the moon which Muslim folk piety associates with the Prophet (cf. Qur'ān *Sūra* 54:1). While this account may have no historical basis, it is, nevertheless, as Yohanan Friedmann has shown, only one of several anecdotes that reflect the widespread tendency among South Asian Muslims to demonstrate both the antiquity and respectability of their association with the Islamic tradition.[1] Indeed, Islam has flourished so well in the Indian subcontinent, that today the region is home to the single largest body of Muslims in the world—there are more Muslims in India, Pakistan, and Bangladesh than in all the Arab countries put together. Furthermore, Muslims from this region have been responsible for spreading their religion to other areas of the world—notably to Southeast Asia and East Africa, and more recently to the Western world, especially the United Kingdom, Canada, and the United States.

Islam in South Asia had rather humble beginnings. As early as the mid-seventh century, a few Arab merchants settled on the southern and western coasts of India to earn a living through trade. Over the next couple of centuries, this small Arab Muslim trading presence grew at a steady rate in the towns of Southern India, proving to be culturally and historically more significant than any Arab military presence. In fact, the Arabs did not seem very interested in conquering large areas in this region. The sole Arab military campaign of any significance took

1. Yohanan Friedmann, "*Qissat Shakarwatī Farmāḍ:* A tradition concerning the introduction of Islam to Malabar," *Israel Oriental Studies* 5 (1975): 233–58.

place in 711 when a small military force under the command of a seventeen-year-old Arab general, Muḥammad ibn al-Qāsim, set out from Iraq to avenge the capture of some Muslim women by local pirates. Though this small Arab force conquered the region of Sind up to the city of Multan, and established a state along the Indus Valley, the Arab presence in this state was so small that they could not impose their religion on a country with a very different culture. On the contrary, Muḥammad ibn al-Qāsim acknowledged the rights of the native Hindu and Buddhist populations to practice their faith as long as they paid their taxes. He thus equated their position under Muslim rule with that of the *ahl al-kitāb* (the people of the Book)—that is, the Jews, Christians, and Sabians, in the Near East. This early Arab presence in Western and Southern India considerably predated the military invasion of Northern India by Turko-Persian Muslim armies in the tenth century. Initially, these Turkish military expeditions into the subcontinent from Central Asia and Afghanistan were quick loot-and-plunder raids that only gradually led to the establishment of permanent Muslim rule in the eleventh century. By the twelfth century, a Turko-Persian dynasty (the Ghorids) had acquired substantial control over the Northern Indian plain conquering cities such as Delhi, Ajmer, and Gwalior. Areas of Bengal were conquered in the beginning of the thirteenth century as were some parts of Assam and Orissa. Towards the end of the thirteenth and the beginning of the fourteenth century, Turko-Persian rulers had expanded Muslim rule not only in western provinces, such as Gujarat, but also down south into the heart of the Deccan. The late fourteenth and early fifteenth centuries witnessed the emergence of several independent Muslim states in Southern and Northern India. Those areas in the south gave rise, in the sixteenth century, to the kingdoms of Bijapur and Golkonda, while those areas in the north consolidated into a single powerful empire under the rule of the Mughals—the most renowned dynasty of Muslim India. Mighty as the Mughal Empire was in its heyday, by the eighteenth century it began to disintegrate rapidly, making it easy for the British to take control of India.

During its twelve-hundred-year presence in the subcontinent, the Islamic tradition has had a profound impact on all aspects of South Asian culture and life. Though it entered the region in a cultural mold that was predominantly Turko-Persian, the tradition also interacted with the indigenous cultures to create a highly sophisticated civilization that we may describe as Indo-Muslim. The more visible and concrete achievements of this civilization are renowned all over the world. The Taj Mahal, the monumental mosques, palaces, forts, and pleasure gardens that dot the subcontinent's landscape, as well as exquisite miniature paintings, are among just a few of the attainments of Indo-Muslim culture in the field of art and architecture. On the one hand this culture is rooted in and intimately connected to the Turko-Persian and Arabic worlds but, on the other, it has developed—because of its Indic cultural base—its own distinct identity. The society it nurtured was splintered into a complex pattern of cleavages along political, social, economic, ethnic, and even religious lines. These fissures are reflected in the countless individuals who represented Indo-Muslim society, whether powerful emperors or humble subjects, landowning aristocrats or exploited tenant farmers, sophisticated urban literati or illiterate peasants, learned religious scholars or popular Ṣūfī saints. Indeed, the heterogeneous Muslim community of South Asia is so fragmented that there seem to be few bonds that hold it together. Perhaps the most powerful of these bonds is allegiance and loyalty to Muḥammad, the Prophet of Islam.

Wilfred Cantwell Smith, commenting on the significance of the prophet Muḥammad for the Muslim community of early twentieth-century India, writes:

> The emphasis is on Muhammad as a person, a human being of commanding excellence. . . . He becomes the object of a devotion, virtually an adoration, that can hardly be exaggerated. . . . Muslims will allow attacks on Allah: there are atheists and atheistic publications, and rationalistic societies; but to disparage Muhammad will provoke from even the most "liberal" sections of the community a fanaticism of blazing vehemence.[2]

Made almost half a century ago, these remarks seem—in light of the Salman Rushdie affair—particularly pertinent to our times. On the one hand, they underscore the centrality of the Prophet in Muslim religious life.[3] For centuries, Muḥammad has provided Muslims all over the world with the paradigm for establishing legal, personal, and social norms for their societies. In the words of the Qur'ān: he is "a beautiful

---

2. W. C. Smith, *Modern Islam in India,* 2d. ed. rev. (Lahore: Muhammad Ashraf, repr. 1969), 72.

3. For a general discussion of the Prophet's role in Muslim piety, see Tor Andrae, *Die Person Muhammeds in Lehre und Glauben seiner Gemeinde* (Stockholm: P. A. Vorstedt og soner, 1918); Constance Padwick, *Muslim Devotions* (London: SPCK, 1960); and Annemarie Schimmel, *And Muhammad Is His Messenger* (Chapel Hill: University of North Carolina Press, 1985) and various articles on the subject by the same author.

model" *(uswa ḥasana)*[4] whose example is to be followed by the faithful. Indeed, according to the Muslim scripture, to obey the Prophet means to obey God.[5] The nature of Muḥammad's mission, sent as he was "as a mercy to the world,"[6] forms the subject of many books and treatises.[7] And a logical corollary of his mercifulness has been his role as intercessor (*shafīʿ*): a role that is, however, not explicitly articulated in the Qurʾān.[8] For Muslims with mystical inclinations, the Prophet's spiritual and mystical status—particularly on account of his mysterious night journey to the highest heaven (*miʿrāj*)—has been subject to much speculation.[9] However lofty such speculation may be, it has always been tempered by the necessity to portray Muḥammad, ultimately, as God's servant *(ʿabd allāh)*. In this manner, by stressing his humanity, the dangers of totally deifying him were avoided.[10]

Professor Smith's observations also, on the other hand, allude to the deep devotion that the Prophet evokes among his followers. As the following reactions to *The Satanic Verses* from Britain's Muslim community (mostly South Asian) poignantly demonstrate, any attack on the Prophet is perceived by many Muslims in intensely personal terms:

What Rushdie has written is far worse to Muslims than if he has raped one's own daughter. *It's an assault on every Muslim's inner being.* . . . Muslims seek Muhammad as the ideal on which to fashion our lives and conduct, and *the Prophet is internalized into every Muslim's heart. It's like a knife being dug into you*— or being raped yourself. (a leader of Britain's Muslim community)

I started reading *[Satanic Verses]* but when I came to the bits about the Prophet, I put it down. *I love the Prophet. I found it hurt me.* It was very degrading, disgraceful. (a sixteen-year-old high school student)

---

4. *Sūra* 33:21.
5. *Sūra* 4:80.
6. *Sūra* 21:107.
7. See, for example, Alhaj Qasim Ali Jairazbhoy, *Muhammad: A Mercy to all the Nations* (London: Luzac, 1937) and Syed Ameer Ali, *The Life and Teachings of Muhammad* or *The Spirit of Islam* (London: n.p., 1897).
8. See Andrae, *Die Person Muhammeds*, 234–44.
9. See A. A. Affifi, "The Story of the Prophet's Ascent *(miʿrāj)* in Sufi Thought and Literature," *Islamic Quarterly* 2 (1955): 23–29; John C. Archer, *Mystical Elements in Mohammed*, repr. ed. (New Haven: Yale University Press, 1980); Earle H. Waugh, "Following the Beloved: Muhammad as Model in the Sufi Tradition," *The Biographical Process*, ed. Frank E. Reynolds and Donald Capps (The Hague and Paris: Mouton, 1976), 63–85; and Schimmel, *And Muhammad Is His Messenger*, 157–75.
10. Schimmel, *And Muhammad Is His Messenger*, 142–43.

He has killed our Prophet. He has killed us all. We just can't explain how much he has hurt Muslims. I would die rather than hear these things and so would our children. (a Muslim crane-driver)[11]

These comments only confirm what Sir Muḥammad Iqbāl (d. 1938), the Muslim poet-philosopher of Indo-Pakistan, declared in a Persian verse many years ago:

> The Prophet's home is in the heart of the Muslim
> The very name of the Prophet is our glory.[12]

In short, love and devotion for the Prophet are the cornerstones of Islamic practice and are marks of its uniqueness. As Constance Padwick points out, a true understanding of Islam as a religion is impossible without an appreciation of the immense love at the heart of the tradition for Muḥammad, God's beloved *(ḥabīb allāh)*.[13] Muslims have shown their love and devotion to their Prophet in many ways, the most common being the recitation of the *ṣalawāt* (the formula for invoking God's blessing on him).[14] They have also expressed it through innumerable poems written in almost every language of the Islamic world. Whether these are the sophisticated compositions of the literati or the folk songs sung by villagers, the poems are equally filled with warm human emotions towards the Prophet. Frequently in these verses, Muḥammad is addressed as if he were alive and affectionately listening to his followers as they seek his help in solving every type of problem, no matter how seemingly mundane.[15]

In her study of poetry in praise of the Prophet, Professor Schimmel observes that the further poets live from Arabia (the Prophet's home-

11. Emphasis mine. These comments, taken from interviews appearing in the British press during 1989, were brought to my attention by Zoe Herzov, recently of Cambridge, Mass., and now of London.

12. *Asrār-i khūdī* (Lahore: n.p., 1915), lines 357–58.

13. Padwick, *Muslim Devotions,* 145.

14. In this they follow the Qur'ānic command in *Sūra* 33:56 which says "Surely Allah and His angels bless the Prophet; O you who believe! call for blessings on him and salute him with a salutation."

15. The tendency to turn to the Prophet in times of difficulty has become so widespread and common in Indo-Muslim folk piety that even popular Indian films dealing with "Islamic" themes portray it. For example, in the movie *Mughal-i Aʿẓam,* the unjustly imprisoned heroine, Anārkalī, who is later condemned to be buried alive in a wall, sings to the Prophet of her tragic plight: *be kas pe karam kījīe, shāh-i madīna* (O King of Medina, be kind to this destitute one).

land), the more eloquent they become in expressing their yearning for the Prophet and their desire to visit his tomb in the city of Medina.[16] She cites, for example, Yunus Emre (ca. 1300), the early Turkish poet, who cries:

> If my Lord would kindly grant it,
> I would go there, weeping, weeping,
> And Muḥammad in Medina
> I would see there, weeping, weeping.[17]

We can perhaps broaden this remark by observing that it is in the poetry written by Muslims in Islamic lands further away from Arabia that we encounter images of Muḥammad that are more romantic and more exotic. Many non-Arab Muslims tend to clothe their devotion to the Prophet in metaphors and symbols taken quite naturally from their indigenous cultures. Consequently, they often surround him with ideas and themes that may have little or no resonance with the prophetology espoused in the official Islam of the religious scholars. Such assimilation of the Prophet to a local environment is most pronounced in the Indian subcontinent—home to the world's largest concentration of Muslims.

Scholarship on Islam in this part of the world has discerned the existence of two major, often antagonistic, strands in the tradition.[18] The first, associated with those Muslims who interpreted their faith more esoterically or mystically, saw nothing wrong in adapting Islam to the local Indian environment, languages, mores, and traditions. Indeed, it is precisely the indigenization of the faith that was instrumental in spreading, so successfully, the fundamental Islamic precepts among the local populations. As part of this process, even the figure of the Prophet was "Indianized" and presented in terms that would be familiar and palatable to Indian audiences. We can cite here, by way of

---

16. Schimmel, *And Muhammad Is His Messenger*, 190.

17. Ibid., 191.

18. See Imtiaz Ahmad, "The Islamic Tradition in India," *Islam and the Modern Age* 12, no. 1 (1981): 44–62; Annemarie Schimmel, "Reflections on Popular Muslim Poetry," *Contributions to Asian Studies* 17 (1982): 17–26; Yohanan Friedmann, "Islamic Thought in Relation to the Indian Context," *Purusartha* 9 (1986): 79–91; Richard Eaton, *Sufis of Bijapur 1300–1700* (Princeton: Princeton University Press, 1978); and S. C. Misra, "Indigenisation and Islamisation in Muslim Society in India," *India and Contemporary Islam*, ed. S. T. Lokhandwalla (Simla: Indian Institute for Advanced Study, 1971).

example, a rather dramatic case from medieval Bengal, where the Prophet became associated with "comparable symbols of the Hindu tradition."[19] From at least the sixteenth century, if not earlier, Bengali Muslim authors of the folk tradition forged an ostensible correspondence between the Islamic concept of prophethood, on the one hand, and the Hindu concept of the *avatāra* (literally "descent," or divine incarnation), on the other. The personality of Muḥammad was made pertinent to the Bengali religious milieu by being presented as the last and most powerful *Kali avatāra* of the Hindu deity Vishnu.[20] In their turn, Hindu deities such as Krishna were conceived as prophets who preceded Muḥammad, the final prophet-*avatāra* sent down by God to humankind. Similarly, at the other end of the subcontinent, in Gujarat and Sind, medieval preacher-saints identified the Prophet with the Hindu god Brahma, and the Prophet's daughter, Fāṭima, with Brahma's daughter, Saraswati.[21]

At great odds with this assimilatist or adaptive strand was a separatistic and law-bound conservative one, which was often represented by the *ashrāf* (the religious and intellectual elite of Islamic society).[22] Conscious of the Muslim community's minority status in a predominantly Hindu milieu, the *ashrāf* were always anxious to prevent Islam from being absorbed and overwhelmed by "an environment which could only be described as an anathema to their cherished ideal of monotheism."[23] To preserve and protect Islam from encroachment by "idolatrous" Indian customs and beliefs, the separatistic strand cultivated an outlook that has been appropriately termed "prophetic-separatistic" or "Mecca-oriented."[24] It looked to Arabia, the heartland of Islam, for determining the cultural and religious norms for the subcontinent's Muslim community. More significantly, it stressed the Arabian

19. Asim Roy, *The Islamic Syncretistic Tradition in Bengal* (Princeton: Princeton University Press, 1983), 95.

20. Ibid., 98.

21. See Azim Nanji, *The Nizari Ismāʿīlī Tradition in the Indo-Pakistan Subcontinent* (Delmar: Caravan Books, 1978); G. Khakee, "The Dasa Avatāra of the Satpanth Ismailis and Imam Shahis of Indo-Pakistan," Ph.D. diss., Harvard University, 1972; Ali Asani, "The Khojas of Indo-Pakistan: The Quest for an Islamic Identity," *Journal of the Institute of Muslim Minority Affairs* 8, no. 1 (1987): 31–41.

22. Imtiaz Ahmad, "The *ashrāf-ajlāf* dichotomy in Muslim social structure in India," *Indian Economic and Social History Review* 3 (1966): 268–78.

23. Friedmann, "Islamic Thought," 79.

24. Schimmel, "Reflections on Popular Muslim Poetry," 19.

character of Islam by evoking the example of Muḥammad, the Arabian Prophet, as the only reliable guide. The Prophet's Arabian background was highlighted—he was Muḥammad, the Meccan, the Medinan, the Hāshimī, the Qurayshī.[25] Indeed, on account of this Arabian emphasis, the epithet "Arab" in reference to the Prophet occurs more frequently in Islamic literature from South Asia than in any other part of the world. Adherence to the way of the Arabian Prophet to the exclusion of non-Islamic Indian elements became so strong in this conservative strand that some of the powerful reformers associated with it identified themselves as following the *ṭarīqa Muḥammadiyya* (the Muhammadan path).[26]

The history of Islam in the Indian subcontinent can quite easily be interpreted within the framework of the dynamic interplay of these two antagonistic strands. However, as much as their philosophies and outlooks differed, it is significant that the Prophet occupied a prominent position in both ideologies. That is because whether he is perceived through an Arabia-tinted or India-tinted glass, loyalty to him—as expressed in the *shahāda* (the Muslim testimony of faith)—is a hallmark of Muslim identity. We must, however, not forget that over the centuries, the majority of the Prophet's followers have chosen to declare their love and devotion to him in poems and songs in their native languages (such as Tamil, Sindhi, Hindi, Bengali, or Urdu), incorporating themes and ideas typically characteristic of Indian poetry in general.

Among the several literary motifs used by composers of *naʿt* (poetry praising the Prophet) two themes, in particular, stand out. The first is the *virahinī* (a loving and yearning young woman, usually a young bride or bride-to-be), who is tormented by the absence of her husband or lord. This motif most likely originated in plaintive songs sung by the village women in periods of separation from their husbands. This symbol and the associated concept of *viraha* (longing in separation) was enthusiastically adopted in almost all the vernacular literatures of India. The *virahinī* enjoyed great popularity in a wide variety of religious contexts where she was often identified as a symbol for the human soul. Such usage is in keeping with Indian literary conventions according to which the human soul is always to be represented as female

25. Annemarie Schimmel, *As Through A Veil: Mystical Poetry in Islam* (New York: Columbia University Press, 1982), 199–200.

26. Schimmel, *And Muhammad Is His Messenger*, 216–38 and "The Golden Chain of 'Sincere Muhammadans,' " *The Rose and The Rock*, ed. B. Lawrence (Durham: Duke University Press, 1979), 104–34.

before a deity who is male.[27] The most renowned use of the *virahinī* in Indian literature occurs in poetry dedicated to the Hindu god Krishna. In this poetry the *gopīs* (cowmaids), and in particular Rādhā, express their longings for union with their elusive beloved. Jain, Sant, and Sikh religious poetry also have their *virahinīs*. Within an Islamic context, the *virahinī* appears in many genres of vernacular Ṣūfī poetry ranging from the romantic epics of Awadh to the folk songs of Punjab and Bengal.[28] Interestingly, such poetry equates the concept of *viraha* with the Ṣūfī concept of *ʿishq* (the burning, consuming longing of the soul for union with God).[29] The woman-soul is also conspicuous in the devotional literature of the subcontinent's Ismaili community, where she yearns for the Shīʿī *Imām*.[30] The use of the *virahinī*, then, in poetry devoted to Muḥammad (the longed-for beloved) is hardly a surprising development.

The second motif commonly associated with the figure of the Prophet is that of rain and/or a rain cloud. This association may seem rather surprising at first glance, but in many cultures rain and its life-sustaining powers have signified the descent of divine or heavenly influences upon earth.[31] In fact, the use of rain, particularly as a symbol of the Prophet's mercy, is a well-attested traditional Islamic literary convention. Since the Qurʾān itself, in two separate verses,[32] refers to both rain and the Prophet as being signs of God's mercy, "it was but natural to compare him [the Prophet] and his power to the life-giving cloud, the quickening rain."[33] Consequently, Islamic literature is re-

---

27. See John Hawley, "Images of Gender in the Poetry of Krishna," *Gender and Religion: On the Complexity of Symbols,* ed. Caroline W. Bynum, Steven Harrell, and Paula Richman (Boston: Beacon Press, 1986), 231–56.

28. See Schimmel, *As Through A Veil,* 152–54 and Ali S. Asani, "Sufi Poetry in the Folk Tradition of Indo-Pakistan," *Religion and Literature* 20, no. 1 (1988): 81–94.

29. Charlotte Vaudeville, "La conception de l'amour divin dans la Padmāvat de Muhammad Jāyasī, *virah* et *ʿishq,*" *Journal Asiatique* 250 (1962): 351–67.

30. See Ali S. Asani, "Bridal Symbolism in Ismāʿīlī Mystical Literature of Indo-Pakistan," *Mystics of the Book,* ed. R. A. Herrera (New York: Peter Lang, 1993), 389–404.

31. See article on "Rain," *Encyclopedia of Religion,* vol. 12 (New York: Free Press, 1986), 201–5.

32. *Sūras* 7:57 and 21:107.

33. Annemarie Schimmel, "The Veneration of the Prophet Muhammad, as Reflected in Sindhi Poetry," *The Saviour God: Comparative Studies in the Concept of Salvation,* ed. S. G. F. Brandon (Manchester: Manchester University Press, 1963), 135.

plete with examples of the Prophet as rain or a beneficent rain cloud. For example, in the *Burda* (the famous Arabic ode to the Prophet) the rain is a metaphor for the Prophet's mercy to those who are without any helper.[34] One of the foremost poets of the Urdu language, Mirzā Ghālib (d. 1869), in his poem honoring the Prophet, refers to him as a "jewel-bearing cloud" *(abr-i gauharbār),* while the most famous poet in Sindhi, Shāh ʿAbd ul-Laṭīf (d. 1752), addresses him as the "cloud of mercy."[35] In Indian culture, however, rain takes on a special significance. Rain is constantly associated with *viraha*—an association that leads W. G. Archer to comment that Indian folk poetry almost always connects sexual frustration with the rains.[36] Thus, in literary genres such as the *bārahmāsā* (songs of the twelve months), as well as the *caumāsā* (songs of the four months of rain), the rainy season is invariably connected with the *virahinī*.[37] The pangs and agonies of being left alone become particularly intense for her during this time of the year. Not infrequently, the *virahinī*'s beloved is, directly or indirectly, associated with dark rain clouds.[38]

Both literary motifs—the *virahinī* and the rain cloud—have a rich literary heritage behind them, which brings with it the potential for interesting poetic minglings. Their immense appeal as metaphors and symbols, no doubt, explains their pervasiveness in Indian literature. The Prophet's panegyrists took advantage of this popularity by exploring different directions in which these motifs could be extended. With this in mind, we turn now to two poets, both equally renowned for their literary skills as well as their piety. One writes in Sindhi, the language of Sind, and chooses the *virahinī* as a vehicle to express his devotion; the other writes in Urdu, the premier literary language for the subcontinent's Muslim community, and focuses on the rain cloud motif.

---

34. Muhammad Bukhari Lubis, *Qaṣīdahs in honor of the Prophet* (Bangi, Malaysia: Penerbit Universiti Kebangsaan Malaysia, 1983), 42.

35. Schimmel, *And Muhammad is His Messenger*, 81–82.

36. W. G. Archer, "Seasonal Songs of the Patna District," *Man in India*, 22 (1942), 232.

37. Charlotte Vaudeville, *Bārahmāsā in Indian Literatures* (Delhi: Motilal Banarsidass, 1986), 27–33.

38. Ibid., 28.

Chapter 2

The Bridegroom Prophet

Beloved, send for this beggar, your little country girl
For God's sake, O Muṣṭafā, my hero, give me courage!
— . . . .
Beloved! put out the fire of *biraha (viraha)* with your own hands.[1]

(27)

This verse, addressed to Muḥammad was written by a male poet from Sind—the region of the subcontinent that came under Muslim rule as early as 711. The composer, ʿAbd ur-Raʾūf Bhaṭṭī (d. 1752) or *ʿāṣī* (the sinner), as he calls himself, ranks among the first poets to write *maulūds* in his native language Sindhi.[2] Technically intended to be poems describing the Prophet's birth, the Sindhi *maulūds* consist of five to ten verses, patterned after traditional Sindhi poetic forms called the *wāʾī* and *kāfī*. *Maulūds* always contain a beginning verse that is repeated as a refrain (*thal*).[3] As with most Indian poetry, the last verse contains the name of the poet who usually takes the opportunity to offer a supplication to the Prophet. According to one Sindhi religious manual *maulūds* are meant to be recited in "a sweet and harmonious voice," either by an individual or a chorus, so that the listener's heart is "correctly guided."[4] To this day, the numerous poems composed by ʿAbd ur-Raʾūf Bhaṭṭī are recited throughout the villages and towns of Sind, not

1. The number in parentheses refers to the poem number in the ʿAbd ur-Rāʾuf Bhaṭṭi section in Nabibakhsh Baloch, ed., *Maulūd* (Hyderabad, Sind: Sindhi Adabi Board, 1961), 5–33.
2. Meman ʿAbd al-Majīd Sindhī, *Sindhī meṅ naʿtīya shāʿirī* (Larkana: Sindhi Adabi Academy, 1980), 121.
3. Ibid., 133.
4. Ibid., 134–35.

only at religious assemblies and gatherings but during weddings, general occasions of rejoicing, and at times of mourning.[5]

ʿAbd ur-Raʾūf Bhaṭṭī wrote under the influence of the North Indian *virahinī* tradition. As illustrated, he beseeches the Prophet in the voice of a humble and unsophisticated woman, "a little country girl," who can no longer bear the painful agony of being separated from her beloved, in this case the Prophet. It is not surprising then, that the language and vocabulary he employs are typical of the idiom of Sindhi women, utilizing linguistic forms such as the diminutive for tender and affectionate address. Only the Prophet, *Muṣṭafā* (the chosen one), can put out the fire of longing that consumes this young lady. The yearning, pining woman is a leitmotif that runs through almost all of Bhaṭṭī's poems addressed to the Prophet. Indeed, she is a standard character in much Sindhi mystical poetry, where she is always interpreted as symbolizing the human soul in its long quest for God. There too, the woman-soul endures much pain and suffering as she burns in divine love, and frequently dies from intense longing. The representation of the soul as a woman in Sindhi poetry is definitely unusual by the standards of Islamic religious poetry from the Arabic- and Persian-speaking Islamic world. In the Arabo-Persian literary tradition, the woman is generally used as a symbol for something that is negative, such as the seductions of the material world.[6] However, the woman-soul—especially in the form of the *virahinī*—is a symbol adopted by many of the subcontinent's Muslim writers as they indigenized their poetry to the literary tastes of their local Indian audiences.

Bhaṭṭī expresses the *virahinī*'s relationship with the Prophet in several different ways. This relationship is one of mutual love—love and mercy being the essence of the Prophet. Muḥammad is described as "love-intoxicated" (48), "compassionate" (47), "filled with mercy" (3), and a "sweet comforting beloved" (65) for whom thousands have sacrificed themselves in yearning like moths (48). Still, this "sweetest of relationships" (1) is painful and soul-consuming for it burns lovers in the fire of *biraha*, a fire which slowly kills:

> Dying from love, those wounded by the prince, weep in yearning
> (73)

5. Baloch, *Maulūd*, 5.

6. Annemarie Schimmel, *Mystical Dimensions of Islam* (Chapel Hill: University of North Carolina Press, 1975), appendix 2, 426–35.

All this longing kills me!
O intercessor, yearning for you is killing me!
(61)

Deep passion for the beloved entered my heart, immediately there followed pain;
O compassionate one, save me now; remove the burdens of *biraha*.
(65)

Out of intense desire to be in his presence, the Prophet's faithful lover is so anxious to visit his mausoleum that the very "love for Medina" is difficult to bear (45).

Remembering, my eyes yearn; every day lovers come into your presence.
The pilgrims, who travel to Arab country, are in love
There, every day, the travellers recite blessings on the master;
The Prophet's lovers weep on the roads;
Journeying on foot, they come with boundless joy.
(69)

The journey itself is gruesome and involves traversing difficult, desolate distances, leading the woman-soul to exclaim:

Would that I would give up my life crawling along the road to Medina!
(52)

But as the *virahinī* approaches her destination, she sees the minarets of the Prophet's mausoleum—a sight that acts as a soothing balm for her tired and burning eyes:

When I saw the minarets of the true master
The fire in my eyes was soothed.
With longing came the thoughts of the intercessor:
Muḥammad has met thousands of pilgrims.
The joys of proximity as I draw near;
The trembling of emotions [as I think of] Aḥmad [Muḥammad] as my companion.
(47)

According to folk belief, a visit to the Prophet's tomb guarantees his intercession; an idea which Tor Andrae points out "moves in an area which is essentially alien to orthodox Islam."[7] Nevertheless, as any contemporary description of a visit to Medina will prove, the Prophet's *Rauẓa* (garden) in Medina to this day signifies an ecstatic moment for many Muslims. Being in the presence of the Prophet, experiencing what Constance Padwick terms the "awe of the Prophet,"[8] is the fulfillment of a life-long dream. It is a highly emotional moment to which South Asian Muslims, in particular, have devoted entire collections of poetry. In these poems, the Prophet's lovers rejoice at being physically present in his city, Medina. On the other hand they also express the painful yearnings they will feel once they depart and are separated from him again.

This love for the Prophet afflicts the *virahinī* like a sickness for which Muḥammad is the only cure:

> I am love-sick: beloved, you be my health!
> The beloved need only come to my house and
> All pains and afflictions will be cured.
>
> (49)

Muḥammad is not only the "medicine of the afflicted" (69) but he is also the physician who can, through his mercy, save a soul dying from love-sickness:

> Revive me so that I may live; otherwise I shall surely die.
> Cure me with the medicines and potions of mercy
> You are the physician and the healer;
> Place your hand on this weak one.
>
> (30)

Yet the most dramatic aspect of the *virahinī* symbol in Bhaṭṭī's work recalls the image of the young bride-to-be and her impending marriage to Muḥammad, the bridegroom of Medina. The poet makes condensed references to a host of terms and images pertaining to weddings in Sindhi society. He uses these to allude to the true nature of the woman-soul's devotion to the Prophet in a form that arouses immediate associations and emotions among his listeners.

Like all Indian weddings, this wedding too, is preceded by a henna

7. Tor Andrae, *Die Person Muhammeds in Lehre und Glaube seiner Gemeinde* (Stockholm: P. A. Vorstedt og soner, 1918), 256.

8. Constance Padwick, *Muslim Devotions* (London: SPCK, 1960), 142.

(meṅhdī) night (when the bride's hands and feet are stained with henna) and at this henna party innumerable angels are present (16). As the hour of the wedding approaches, the ladies of the household have climbed on the upper storeys of the house to catch a glimpse of the bridegroom as he arrives (6). Meanwhile the bride anxiously awaits her bridegroom Prophet. In typical Sindhi fashion, he comes wearing a turban of honor, the turban of faith, tied on him by God Himself (16). He arrives riding a horse—a well-harnessed horse (14) with a golden saddlecloth (10)—or on a camel (6). The waiting bride-soul exclaims:

> O girlfriends! The handsome, beloved bridegroom has come!
>
> (8)

The procession accompanying the Prophet is comprised of heavenly beings. There are ten million attending angels (9) who distribute musk and perfume to the populace (12). At the same time, they shower Muḥammad with flowers and rose petals (15) as well as precious gems (8). The *ḥūr*s (the paradisiacal virgins) rejoice noisily (10) while making garlands (16), bearing wedding gifts (14), and showering the bridegroom with millions of rubies (11). A fragrant wedding bed, on which the angels have scattered pearls (14), has been prepared for the bridegroom. Finally, the groom sits on the bed (13) and leans against the cushions on which are scattered roses (10). Now the bride-soul knows that her desire to meet the Prophet-bridegroom will be fulfilled:

> The lord sat on the bed, on which lie scattered pearls
> Thanks be to God! the wedding will take place.
>
> (13)

By representing the Prophet as a bridegroom, the poet Bhaṭṭī utilizes a symbol that has become a distinctive feature of many Sindhi panegyrics. Bhaṭṭī employs another literary device, equally fashionable in Sindhi poetry—the use of folk tales and romances as allegories. The culture of Sind is so permeated with folk tales and romances that a scholar of Sindhi literary history considers them to be a pivot around which the bulk of Sindhi literature revolves, regardless of form or theme.[9] In keeping with this tradition, Bhaṭṭī too, makes allusions to

9. L. H. Ajwani, *History of Sindhi Literature* (Karachi: Allied Book Co., 1984), 40.

Sindhi romances in his works. He does not narrate these romances for he assumes his listeners are well aware of their details. He only judiciously refers to those tales that feature a *virahinī*. In this way he continues to preserve a consistency in his symbolism.

A particularly favorite tale of his is the Sassui-Puṅhuṅ romance. The story has a simple plot: Sassui, the adopted daughter of a washerman, was the boast and beauty of the town of Bhambhore, and a considerable sensation in society. Puṅhuṅ, a handsome Balochi prince, much to the distress of his noble father and brothers not only falls in love with Sassui but stays with her family as a lowly washerman until he finally gets to marry her. Outraged by his behavior, Puṅhuṅ's brothers, through force and stratagem, manage to kidnap a very drunk Puṅhuṅ from Sassui as she lays peacefully asleep. On awakening, the deserted bride is heartbroken and desolate. She sets out, alone, in pursuit of her beloved on a fatal two-hundred-mile march across a dreadful desert and still more dreadful hills.[10]

For Bhaṭṭī, the heroine Sassui is the *virahinī*, separated from her beloved Puṅhuṅ. She represents the soul who longs to meet the beloved Prophet (in this case Puṅhuṅ), ready to undergo all trials and affliction in the process. Addressing the Prophet as Puṅhal (an affectionate form of Puṅhuṅ) Bhaṭṭī's Sassui cries:

> Dear sweetheart, I will not forget my beloved, the Prophet
> For you, I spread my hair as a mat, O Puṅhal, my prince!
> Beloved, more fragrant than musk and ambergris is your sweat;
> On account of your beauty, the moon sacrifices itself.
>
> (5)

Bhaṭṭī also alludes to Sassui's arduous journeys in quest of her beloved:

> Remembering, my little heart longs for the beloved [Puṅhuṅ]
> Difficult, desolate distances, dear Puṅhuṅ makes me travel!
> O Generous One, show me the tomb of the Prophet.
>
> (45)

10. This summary of the Sassui-Puṅhuṅ romance is closely based on Sir Richard Burton's rather colorful account in *Sind Revisited: With notices of the Anglo-Indian army; railroads; past, present and future*, vol. 1 (London: R. Bentley and Son, 1877), 129–32.

I pluck roses along the roadside so that I may welcome Puṅhuṅ when he comes.
How many tasks shall I undertake for the sake of Puṅhal?
The journeys are dangerous and difficult, escort me across safely!
May the Generous One show me the mausoleum of the Prophet.
(58)

In another poem, Bhaṭṭī tries to capture Sassui's agony and pain as she awakens from her sleep to find Puṅhuṅ has disappeared. She is beside herself with grief and there is no reason for her to stay in her town, Bhambhore, any longer. She is determined to set out in pursuit of him, even if it means being ground by the "fist of death" (71). Though the Puṅhuṅ of folklore was ethnically a Balochi, Bhaṭṭī's Puṅhuṅ, of course, represents the Prophet. Hence he is addressed as Hāshimī (coming from the Banu Hāshim, the Arabian clan of the Prophet).

O girlfriends! How can I bear this? I, who am walking towards the beloved Puṅhuṅ
While awake, I weep; while sleeping, I have no peace;
Thoughts of the Hashimite friend overcome me!
Sisters, staying in this Bhambhore is poison to me!
The fist of death grinds me along the road;
Seizing me by the roots, love has carried me away!
The grasped hem no longer remains [in my hands]; I live but my life is gone!
The "sinner" ʿAbd ar-Raʾūf says, "Treat me kindly:
I am going to the Prince of Medina and I will return."
(71)

To relieve the despondency and gloom of the Sassui tale, Bhaṭṭī also refers to another romance, this one with a more happy ending. It is the tale of Prince Jām Tamāchī, who falls in love with the charming, but lowly, fishermaid Nūrī. The heroine in this tale is interpreted as nothing less than the symbol of the perfect and obedient soul who pleases her lord (the Prophet). Her mighty but loving lord in return covers her, and all who belong to her, with loving kindness.[11] We have here a situation that fulfills the *virahinī*'s most ardent desire—a state of

11. Annemarie Schimmel, *Pain and Grace: A Study of Two Mystical Writers of Eighteenth Century Muslim India* (Leiden: E. J. Brill, 1976), 175.

marital bliss *(suhāg)* in which the lover and beloved, Nūrī and Tamāchī, the yearning soul and the loving Prophet, are happily united.

> O you, medicine for the little sinners and aggrieved ones,
> Muḥammad, the bridegroom of Medina.
> When Samo [Jām Tamāchī][12] was born, peace prevailed; wealth descended on nations.
> Happy in the marital bliss *(suhāg)* of the Prince's affections, oh, the fisherwomen smile:
> On the shores of the Kīnjhar lake,[13] they talk about love!
>
> (4)

12. Meaning here the prophet Muḥammad.
13. A pond near Thatta in Sind, which abounds in fish.

Chapter 3

The Rain Cloud and the Prophet

Among all the Urdu/Hindi poems exalting the Prophet, none has been more renowned for its use of the rain cloud imagery than Muḥsin Kākorawī's *Madīḥ khair al-mursalīn* (Eulogy for the best of messengers). Beginning with the dramatic line, *simt-i Kāshī se ćalā jānib-i Mathrā bādal* (from the direction of Benares went a cloud toward Mathura), this poem has inspired many imitations. Its composer, Muḥsin Kākorawī (d. 1905), was a member of an *ʿalawī sayyid*[1] family whose ancestors were guardians of the Prophet's tomb in Medina. Though professionally a lawyer, Kākorawī ranks as the first major Urdu poet to dedicate himself to composing solely *naʿts* (poems praising the Prophet). As he put it:

> When blessings were distributed in pre-eternity,
> The art of [writing] *naʿt* was assigned to my tongue.[2]

Composing his very first panegyric at the tender age of nine, after the Prophet appeared to him in a dream,[3] Muḥsin Kākorawī remained faithful to a declaration he once made to the Prophet:

> It is my desire that none of my poetry
> should be devoid of your *naʿt*.[4]
> (121)

1. Descendants of the Prophet through his son-in-law, ʿAlī, and daughter, Fāṭima.
2. Muhammad Nūr al-Ḥasan, *Kulliyyāt-i naʿt-i Muḥsin Kākorawī* (Lucknow: Uttar Pradesh Urdu Academy, 1982), 2.
3. Ibid., 8–9.
4. The number in parentheses indicates the page number on which the verse occurs in Nūr al-Ḥasan, *Kulliyyāt-i naʿt-i Muḥsin Kākorawī.*

His poetry achieved widespread fame and popularity, so much so that one religious scholar even had a dream in which the Prophet endorsed the recitation of Muḥsin Kākorawī's verse since Muḥammad, himself, found it to be "very good and pleasing."[5]

From the literary point of view, the poem *Madīḥ khair al-mursalīn* is particularly unusual for its charming combination of verse styles, imagery, and vocabulary drawn extensively from the Indian as well as the Perso-Arabic traditions. It exhibits a rather exceptional blending of the indigenous with the foreign, and the popular with the classical. In this, it represents a bold experiment by its composer to depart from the conventions and norms of classical Urdu poetry. Not too surprisingly, Muḥsin Kākorawī was severely criticized for the daring and unconventional nature of this poem. This criticism, however, did little to detract from his universally acknowledged status as the Prophet's foremost panegyrist in Urdu. For his lifelong veneration of the Prophet, Kākorawī was popularly known as *Ḥassān-i waqt* (the Ḥassān of his time). This title is an allusion to Ḥassān ibn Thābit, the Prophet's Arab eulogist in the seventh century.

Structurally, "Eulogy for the best of messengers" is a long *qaṣīda*[6]—the verse form conventionally employed to write panegyrics in Arabic, Persian, and related languages (such as Turkish and Urdu). The whole composition can be scanned mercilessly in the Perso-Arabic meter *ramal muthamman*[7] with a monorhyme ending in a consonant, short "a" vowel, and the consonant "l" as in *bādal, jal, gokal.* Like a traditional *qaṣīda,* it is divided into three parts. The first is the *tashbīb* (the exordium or introduction), the main function of which is to permit the poet to capture the attention of listeners. This is usually accomplished by introducing erotic or amatory subjects—though descriptions of nature and geographical regions are also found. The *tashbīb* is followed by the *madḥ* (the central portion of the *qaṣīda*) in which the poet displays his/her skills in praising his/her patron, in Kākorawī's case the Prophet. Finally, the *qaṣīda* ends with the *duʿā* (the petition or prayer) in which the poet presents his/her humble requests to his/her patron.

It is the poem's first part, the *tashbīb,* that is most interesting and the most controversial. In its meter and rhyme it is perfectly conventional.

5. Ibid., 31.

6. This also includes a couple of small *ghazals* within the framework of the *qaṣīda.*

7. The arrangement of syllables in this meter is as follows:
– ⏑ ⏑ | – – ⏑ ⏓ | – – ⏑ ⏑ | – – ⏑ ⏓.

However, its imagery as well as its vocabulary may appear peculiar, especially for a *qaṣīda* on an Islamic theme. The very first verse *(bayt)* can have a startling effect on listeners because of the clear Hindu nuances:

> From the direction of Benares went a cloud toward Mathura
> The breeze brings Ganges water on the shoulders of lightning.
>
> (95)

Both Benares and Mathura are important pilgrimage sites in the Hindu tradition—Benares is the most sacred of all cities for Hindus, while Mathura is held in great honor as the birthplace and early residence of Krishna. The significance of the water (in the form of rain) from the Ganges—the most sacred river of the Hindus—becomes apparent in subsequent verses. The rain cloud showers the residents of Gokal—a tract of the river Jumna which served as the residence of Krishna during his youth—with this holy water, and makes them pure. The poet then declares:

> News has just reached the great forest that
> The wind-borne clouds are coming to the pilgrimage sites.
>
> (95)

These are no ordinary clouds. According to the poem many such dense, black rain clouds have filled the sky. They are the clouds of infidelity—the color black being associated with Hindus and infidelity in the Persian-influenced Urdu literary tradition.[8] It seems:

> The idols hold sway not only in Hind [India] but indeed the whole world.
>
> (95)

The clouds slowly move eastwards in the direction of the Kaᶜba, which in pre-Islamic times served as a temple of the infidel pagans. The poet warns:

---

8. For a detailed discussion of this symbolism, and especially association of the color black with the Hindu, see Annemarie Schimmel, "Turk and Hindu: A Poetical Image and Its Application to Historical Fact," *Islam and Cultural Change in the Middle Ages*, ed. Speros Vryonis, Jr. (Wiesbaden: Harrassowitz, 1975), 107–26.

Perhaps Lāt and Hubal[9] may yet again lay siege on the Kaʿba.

(96)

Such is the opening scene described in the first seven verses of this panegyric to the prophet Muḥammad. The Indian and Hindu themes continue as the poem takes on the character of an Indian rain song describing the onset of the rainy season. The rains of Bhādoṇ (the month of rains in the Hindu calendar) are heavy and continuous, spreading the flood waters of the Ganges River everywhere. The gusts of wind overturn the boats which come out filled with Ganges water *(gangā jal)*. The complex of images associated with the rainy season in Indian literature also always involves the theme of *viraha* and the yearnings of a lonely wife (the *virahinī*). So quite appropriately the *gopīs* (the cowmaids), who lovingly pine for their lord Krishna, make their appearance. And as in many popular Hindu devotional poems, the *gopīs*, with their hearts beating restlessly in their constricted bosoms, wonder:

How will we be blessed with the *darshan* (vision) of Lord Krishna?

(97)

Indian rain songs always describe the days of the rainy season as dark and dreary.[10] In keeping with this convention, this poem, too, turns to darkness. The darkness is so overwhelming that neither the moon can be seen at night nor the sun during the day (99). In the blinding darkness, the clouds themselves cannot move, and, amazingly, the moth seeking to immolate itself has to search for the candle flame with the help of a torch (99)! The poet, to further develop the equation of darkness with infidelity, introduces Layla, the symbol of divine beauty in Arabic and Persian mystical poetry. Since her name is connected with the Arabic word for night (*layl*), the poet, in a multiple pun, declares that if Layla were to reveal her face by lifting her veil, the lover would witness only infidelity (darkness) on account of it being too dark for him to see (98). As he puts it, the infidel has applied lampblack (the color symbolizing infidelity) in the eye of infidelity (98). This means that darkness has been compounded by further darkness; that is, infidelity permeates everything and everywhere.

As the *tashbīb* continues, the identity of this dark cloud becomes clear:

---

9. The names of pre-Islamic Arab deities.

10. Charlotte Vaudeville, *Bārahmāsā in Indian Literatures* (Delhi: Motilal Banardsidass, 1986), 36.

Today in Braj the Lord Krishna is the black cloud
The cloud that casts a good [protective] shadow over Gokal and Mathura.
Today the cloud is immersed in the color of Kanhaiya [Krishna].
(104)

As in a typically well-written *qaṣīda,* the *tashbīb* contains several other beautifully concocted images, many of them very cleverly manipulated to demonstrate the composer's command over the language. But it is the Indian and Hindu themes, and their predominance in this portion of the panegyric, that aroused criticism among Muḥsin Kākorawī's contemporaries. These critics were obviously disturbed by his attempt to "Indianize" and popularize a classical *qaṣīda* on such a significant Islamic topic. Was it appropriate for a poet of Muḥsin Kākorawī's heritage and stature to employ expressions and idioms from Hindi: a language which, on account of its Sanskrit-based vocabulary, they identified as belonging to the Hindus?[11] Was it fitting that a *qaṣīda* in praise of the Prophet of Islam should contain references to a Hindu deity (Krishna) and mention Hindu sacred places (such as Mathura, Gokal)?

Amīr Mināī, a friend and contemporary of the composer, argues in Muḥsin Kākorawī's defense that no one has laid down any literary rules governing the topics that may or may not be addressed in the *tashbīb* (exordium). Though certain subjects have traditionally been associated with this section of the *qaṣīda*—days of youth, erotic and amatory subjects—poets have by no means been restricted to them. Significantly, he strengthens his argument by evoking the example of the *Bānat Suʿād,* the most popular Arabic *qaṣīda* written in praise of the Prophet, composed by Kaʿb ibn Zuhayr, a former antagonist of the Prophet. When this Arabic panegyric, which also had an unconventional *tashbīb,* was recited in front of Muḥammad, he had nothing but praise for its beauty.[12]

Muḥsin Kākorawī, himself, upset at the criticism, wrote a poetic defense in which he claimed that to truly appreciate the poem, it should be considered in its entirety "with the eye of justice." Then, it would be quite obvious that the infidelity portrayed in the first section comes to a happy end in the affirmation of faith—that is, in Islam and the

11. For a discussion on the reluctance of Indo-Muslim literati to write on Islamic subjects in Indic vernacular languages (which they considered "vulgar" and "substandard"), see Ali S. Asani, "Amir Khusraw and Poetry in Indic Languages," *Islamic Culture,* 62, 2–3 (1988): 50–62.

12. Nūr al-Ḥasan, *Kulliyāt-i naʿt,* 93.

Prophet. Moreover, he claims, it is customary for the poets of Islam to compare infidelity with darkness, and faith with light—which is precisely what he does in this composition. Significantly, he also turns to prophetic example for endorsement of his case when he points out that Muḥammad, himself, expressed his pleasure with the *Bānat Suʿād* (which describes him as the light that illuminates).[13]

As both Muḥsin Kākorawī and Amīr Mināī suggest, in the *madḥ* (praise) section, there is a dramatic change in the mood and style of the *qaṣīda*. Linguistically, the vocabulary switches from Hindi and Sanskrit based terms to a heavy use of Arabic and Persian terminology and constructions. This linguistic change is accompanied by a change in subject as the Prophet is praised and terms and concepts associated with Islamic belief prevail. Changes can also be discerned in the style, which becomes pompous and grandiose. For example, while extolling the Prophet, the poet declares:

> Your metaphor[ical] being is a matter of astonishment for reality
> Your supplication is the place of coquetry for self-sufficiency.
>
> (117)

The poet shows off his poetic skills by drawing on the full range of rhetorical devices, including allusions to the Qurʾān and the *ḥadīth*, to praise the Prophet. It is amusing to note that at one point, Muḥsin Kākorawī modestly declares that he would write many more befitting verses for the Prophet but his pen would become ecstatic and fly off from his hand (114)!

In regards to imagery, the *madḥ* clearly shows the influence of the *sabk-i hindī* (the Indian style of Persian poetry), the impact of which was also felt on classical Urdu literature. This style is characterized by the compression of a world of meaning into a single image; the employment in unexpected ways of familiar and conventional symbols, so that they never retain a fixed meaning; and the use of artificially created and abstruse diction, often so strange that even an educated native speaker would find the poetry difficult to follow.

The *madḥ* proper begins with the reintroduction of the cloud, now a symbol of the Prophet, as it journeys to the highest heaven—a reference to the Prophet's own heavenly ascension *(miʿrāj)*. The cloud, having witnessed divine light, is praised with the honorific title "one who is consumed by the sudden lightning of [divine] manifestation" (111). As the poet begins to describe various heavenly sites and, then, turns to high-flown and glowing praise of the Prophet's various attributes

13. Ibid., 94.

and uniqueness, the symbol of the cloud falls into the background. However, he returns to the cloud symbol several verses later when he breaks the *qaṣīda* with a *ghazal* (love-lyric) using the rhyme-word *bādal* (cloud). Muḥsin Kākorawī, a faithful adherent of the *sabk-i hindī* style, delights in playing with the cloud symbol, ever attaching new meanings to it. It is a faithful cloud, having left behind India, the land of infidelity:

How [beautifully] the cloud prostrates towards the Kaʿba, the *qibla;*
The cloud prostrates towards Yathrib [Medina] and Baṯḥā [a valley near Medina].
Having abandoned the tavern of India and the idol house of Braj,
Today the cloud has spread its prayer rug in the Kaʿba.
(118)

At the same time, the cloud continues to function as a prophetic symbol: it is a special mercy of the Lord Almighty (118); on account of its blackness the cloud becomes the black hair of the Prophet (119); Jesus declares it to be unique just as Muḥammad is unique (119); like the Prophet, the cloud came before the exalted throne on the night of the *miʿrāj,* in the verdant meadow of the world above (119); and finally, the cloud represents the Prophet's generosity—it is the hand in the rose garden of generosity (120). In other contexts, the cloud = prophet symbolism becomes obscure with the cloud appearing to be a helper or assistant of the Prophet. For example, the cloud brings the Prophet "the grey horse of the heavens" (118) or it spreads the news of his prophethood (120). But, however much Muḥsin Kākorawī plays with the cloud symbol, one point is clear: in the *madḥ,* the cloud becomes a positive symbol of the true faith of Islam, just as much as it was a negative symbol of infidelity in the *tashbīb.*

It is fitting that the cloud symbol appears one final time at the beginning of the *duʿā* (petition) as it comes around to gather supplications like a prophet. The *duʿā* contains some very beautiful and touching verses declaring the poet's total dependance and reliance on the Prophet's kindness and generosity:

Only on you do I depend, on your strength, on your power.
May [you be] my fibre of hope and palm tree, fresh and green.[14]
Whose every branch has flowers, and whose every flower contains a fruit.
(121)

---

14. This is an allusion to the Qurʾānic story of Mary, who was supported by the trunk of the palm tree and its fruit as she gave birth to Jesus. *Sūra* 19: 23–26.

The poet desires the name of the Prophet be on his lips as he dies, so that the Prophet may intercede for him. He wants concealed in his heart the secret of *bilā mīm* (without m), the secret of the Prophet's spiritual status (122).[15]

So strong is the poet's confidence and trust in the Prophet's intercession that he portrays his last moments quite cheerfully and nonchalantly. The angel of death lovingly asks the poet whether he wants to come along to Medina, the Prophet's city. He is reassuringly told:

> Don't worry about the day of resurrection, we'll take care of it tomorrow.
> (122)

And Munkar and Nakīr, the two scribe angels whose job it is to record a person's deeds, welcome him with the words:

> Feel at home [here]; don't be distressed, don't be anxious!
> (122)

But Muḥsin's love for the Prophet extends, in his conception, even to the after-life. He hopes that he will continue to praise the Prophet there. Perhaps the angel Gabriel, on the day of resurrection, will command Muḥsin to recite this very *qaṣīda* by telling him:

> Yes, begin in the name of God,
> "From the direction of Benares went a cloud towards Mathura."
> (123)

In this skillful manner, Muḥsin Kākorawī ends his poem with exactly the same hemistich with which he began.

The two poets we have looked at in this chapter represent two very different dimensions of Islamic South Asia. ʿAbd ar-Raʾūf Bhaṭṭī, the Sindhi, is heavily influenced by the culture and traditions of rural Sind. He belongs to a poetic tradition that is deeply rooted in folk poetry (especially the popular tradition of women's songs). He employs the structure of regional folk poetry and local imagery to create poems that

---

15. This is an allusion to the *ḥadīth qudsī* (divine saying), extremely popular in eastern Islamic lands, according to which God declared: *Anā Aḥmad bilā mīm*, "I am Aḥmad [that is, Muḥammad] without the [letter] m [which means *aḥad*, "One," a reference to God's unity]." The letter "m," symbolizing the Prophet, is in Islamic numerology equivalent to 40, the number of stages, according to some mystics, separating humanity from the Divine.

may not be literary masterpieces. Nevertheless, they are effective in transmitting his message within a regional context in a regional idiom. His symbols for the Prophet are also local, simple to understand, and are not burdened with too many theoretical speculations. The Prophet Bhaṭṭī portrays is all too human—like a kind and loving bridegroom for a bride. Bhaṭṭī is a poet whose poetry comes from the heart and appeals to the emotions of a wide audience, both rural and urban.

Muḥsin Kākorawī, on the other hand, is a product of the sophisticated urban Islamic culture of Northern India. The culture is Indian but at the same time heavily influenced in its tastes by centuries of contact with the Turko-Persian Islamic culture of Central Asia and Iran. It was a civilization associated with a Muslim ruling elite (of foreign ancestry) with lifestyles very different from rural Sind. In its literary tastes, this elite preferred the embellishments and intricacies of Persian-influenced poetic style. Much of Muḥsin Kākorawī's poetry clearly caters to the literary tastes of this aristocratic culture—for only a person thoroughly versed in it could fully appreciate the niceties of his poetic style. It is perhaps because of his style and cultural background that his portrayal of the Prophet tends to be metaphysical and transcendental. At the same time, however, Muḥsin Kākorawī tried to break through the literary conventions of this culture by trying to indigenize (as far as he could) the language and symbolism of his poetry to an Indian milieu. In the process, he, too, drew on the language and the imagery of the Indian tradition so that his poetry, by marrying the popular with the classical, could appeal to a wider audience. That his *Madīḥ khair al-mursalīn* (Eulogy for the best of messengers) remains a favorite to this day is a testimony to the success of his experiment.

Whatever differences exist in the backgrounds of these two poets and their audiences, we can discern in their attitudes to the Prophet, manifest in different idioms, the same enthusiastic love and devotion. Love of the Prophet is a powerful reconciler of differences and a force for communal unity. As Sir Muḥammad Iqbāl, the poet-philosopher of Indo-Pakistan, says in his poem *Rumūz-i bekhudī:* it runs like blood in the veins of the Muslim community.[16]

16. *Rumūz-i bekhūdī* (Lahore: n.p., 1917), 190.

PART 2

THE PROPHET MUḤAMMAD IN AN EGYPTIAN NARRATIVE BALLAD

CHAPTER 4

Introduction

We have seen thus far the portrayals of the figure of the prophet Muḥammad in Indo-Muslim poetry, in both the folk poetry of rural Sind and in the sophisticated poetry of urban Islamic culture of Northern India, and how these portrayals draw on a plethora of indigenous and borrowed poetic imagery and forms. In part 2 we move to another Islamic context with a totally different historical and cultural character. We will examine the portrayal of the Prophet of Islam in the popular poetry of modern Egyptian Muslims.

We have chosen Egypt because of its central role in Islamic and Arab history. Since Egypt was conquered by the Muslim army in the year 639, it became one of the first Islamic states, playing a leading role in the Muslim world—especially after the fall of Baghdad to the Mongols and the end of the ʿAbassid caliphate in 1250. With its millenary mosque/university al-Azhar, Egypt has been a major Islamic cultural center and home to a number of outstanding Islamic figures: commanders such as the famed Ṣalāḥ ad-Dīn al-Ayyūbī (Saladin), who scored a victory over the Crusaders and wrested Jerusalem from Christian control in 1187; legal authorities such as Imām ash-Shāfiʿī (d. 822); historians like al-Maqrīzī (d. 1442) and the Tunisian-born Ibn Khaldūn (d. 1406); and reformers like Muḥammad ʿAbduh (d. 1905).

Egypt could also boast of a number of poets who have enriched Arabic literature and who have particularly contributed to the fund of mystical Ṣūfī poetry and the poetry in praise of the prophet Muḥammad—known as *al-madāʾiḥ an-nabawiyya.* In the mystical Ṣūfī poetry, one must mention the Egyptian poet ʿUmar ibn al-Fāriḍ (d. 1235)[1]

1. On Ibn al-Fāriḍ, see among others Issa J. Boullata, "Verbal Arabesque and Mystical Union: A Study of Ibn al-Fāriḍ's Al-Tāʾiyya al-Kubrā," *Arab Studies Quarterly* 3, 2 (1981), 152–69.

whose accomplished mystical odes are still chanted by contemporary Egyptian Ṣūfī singers.[2] Another Egyptian poet, the thirteenth-century Sharaf ad-Dīn al-Būṣīrī (d. 1296), composed the "Mantle Ode" *(al-Burda)* which is perhaps the most famous Arabic eulogy in honor of the prophet Muḥammad. This eulogy has been imitated, enlarged, and quoted by numerous poets from all over the Islamic world.[3] At present, it continues to be chanted in Egyptian religious ceremonies and one can even purchase recordings of it on cassette tapes in many outlets in Egypt.[4]

The "Mantle Ode" was composed by al-Būṣīrī while he was afflicted by paralysis. We are told al-Būṣīrī recited the ode several times, pleaded with God to cure him, and upon falling asleep saw the prophet Muḥammad in a dream. To show his approval of the ode and its author, the Prophet threw his mantle on al-Būṣīrī, who woke to find himself cured. This story is why for a long time the ode was believed to have miraculous healing powers.[5]

Eulogies in honor of the Prophet have continued to be composed in Egypt from the age of al-Būṣīrī to the present time as a testimony to the centrality of the figure of Muḥammad in the minds of Egyptian Muslims. Unfortunately, only the eulogies composed by poets in classical or modern standard Arabic have been collected and studied;[6] whereas the popular eulogies which are couched in colloquial Egyptian Arabic have been sadly neglected. There are no major works devoted solely to the Egyptian folk songs and narrative ballads about the prophet Muḥammad. There are some works, however, which touch on aspects which are germane to our topic: Tor Andrae's *Die Person Muhammeds in Lehre und Glauben seiner Gemeinde* (1918), which studies

---

2. See Earle Waugh, *The Munshidīn of Egypt: Their World and Their Song* (Columbia, S.C.: University of South Carolina Press, 1989), especially 104–36.

3. Annemarie Schimmel, *And Muhammad Is His Messenger* (Chapel Hill: University of North Carolina Press, 1985), 183.

4. In September 1989 Kamal Abdel-Malek purchased in Cairo a cassette tape of the "*Burda*" chanted by one Shaykh al-ʿAṭawānī.

5. See Schimmel, *And Muhammad Is His Messenger,* 183.

6. See Zakī Mubārak, *al-Madāʾiḥ an-Nabawiyya fī l-Adab al-ʿArabī* (Cairo: Muṣṭafā l-Bābī al-Ḥalabī, 1935); Muḥammad Ḥamūda ʿAbd ar-Raḥmān, *al-Madāʾiḥ an-Nabawiyya fī l-ʿAṣr al-Ḥāḍir wa Atharuhā fī l-Adab al-ʿArabī,* M.A. thesis, al-Azhar University, 1967; Yūsuf an-Nabhānī, *al-Majmūʿa an-Nabhāniyya fī l-Madāʾiḥ an-Nabawiyya,* 4 vols. (Beirut: al-Maṭbaʿa al-Adabiyya, 1903; reprinted in Beirut, n.d.).

the development of the figure of Muḥammad in popular Muslim lore; Professor Annemarie Schimmel's *And Muhammad Is His Messenger* (1985), which studies the popular images of the Prophet in Muslim piety; Pierre Cachia's *Popular Narrative Ballads of Modern Egypt* (1989), which studies the different themes and forms of Egyptian narrative ballads (including folk poetic embroideries about the lives of the Prophet and Muslim saints); and Earle Waugh's *The Munshidīn of Egypt* (1989), which studies the worldview of some Ṣūfī chanters and the importance of the figure of Muḥammad.

The neglect of compositions in the colloquial should not be surprising since the overwhelming majority of Arab scholars, as well as orientalists, habitually define Arabic literature as encompassing only the literary works written in standard Arabic—a language which has maintained, by and large, the syntax of the language of the Qurʾān (if not its vocabulary). Works composed in the colloquial and regional dialects have remained outside the pale of the formal elitist literature. Such dialectal literature—whether oral or pen-and-paper compositions—has suffered much neglect if not outright contempt. "Anything expressed in the colloquial," says Pierre Cachia, "when not openly scorned was looked at as mere entertainment; more often than not the text went unrecorded, the artistry unrecognized, the author unremembered."[7]

Narrative ballads are dismissed as the ravings of an illiterate and superstitious folk. In the words of von Grunebaum, these popular compositions are "lengthy and repetitious tales [that] lack the dignity that would qualify them for my notice, the Arabic being overly simple not to mention defective, their imagery vulgar, and their composition disheveled."[8] It is hoped that by the end of this chapter we will have amply demonstrated that such notions are patently erroneous.

One should note however, that the neglect and contempt which many Arab and Western scholars have shown towards the dialectal literature are symptomatic of a larger problem that has beset the field of Arabic and Islamic studies: the excessive preoccupation with the texts—which are almost always written in classical Arabic—rather than the local contexts. The recorded tract on the faith rather than the faith as lived, practiced, and expressed by the believers has been the hallmark of Islamic and Arabic scholarly work. But focusing on the re-

7. Pierre Cachia, "The Career of Mustafa Ibrahim ʿAjaj," *Journal of Maltese Studies* 2 (1977), 110.

8. As cited by B. Connelly, *Arab Folk Epic and Identity* (Berkeley: University of California Press, 1986), 3.

corded formal discourse of the educated Muslim elite can only prejudice the scholar against the Muslim masses, who are overwhelmingly unlettered and who live, experience, and express their faith in folk conventions of their own. To ignore these people and their cultural expressions is to cut oneself off from "facts on the ground" and to hover endlessly around the lonely peaks of the formal "high tradition." To veer away from such prejudice against the Muslim folk tradition is to recognize, as Charles Adams put it, "that the reality of religion has its locus in the experience of the devotee and that scholars must, above all else, subject themselves to that experience."[9]

The popular eulogies are chanted by a professional singer called a *maddāḥ* (plural *maddāḥīn*) during religious ceremonies or festivals—especially at the festival which marks the anniversary of the Prophet's birthday *(al-maulid)*. The *maddāḥīn* divide these eulogies into several types:[10]

Ḥunūn: Songs in honor of departing or returning pilgrims.

Taʿṭīrat Maulid: Passages in semirhymed prose recited on the occasion of the Prophet's birthday.

Mawwāl: Narrative ballads which recount episodes in the life of the Prophet.

We will devote the following pages to an in-depth analysis of a long Egyptian popular narrative ballad *(mawwāl)*[11] which deals with the Prophet's trading journey to Syria and his marriage to Khadīja, his first wife. The ballad was chosen because of its range of themes and imagery and, more importantly, because it has long been part of the repertoire of the modern Egyptian *maddāḥīn*.

The ballad was recorded in Cairo in 1938 by the German orientalist, Enno Littmann. The transcribed text, along with a German translation, was published in Denmark in 1950 under the title, *Mohammed im Volksepos: Ein Neuarabisches Heilgenlied*.[12] Recently we obtained an undated

9. See Charles Adams' preface in Richard C. Martin, *Approaches to Islam in Religious Studies* (Tucson: University of Arizona Press, 1985), ix.

10. As recorded in the archives of the *Markaz al-Funūn ash-Shaʿbiyya* (Center for Folk Arts) in Cairo.

11. On the *mawwāl*, see Pierre Cachia's excellent study *Popular Narrative Ballads of Modern Egypt* (Oxford: Oxford University Press, 1989).

12. Enno Littmann, *Mohammed Im Volksepos: Ein Neuarabisches Heilingenlied* (Copenhagen: Ejnar Munksgaard, 1950). Some brief references to the ballad can be found in Pierre Cachia's *Popular Narrative Ballads of Modern Egypt*, 19, 35, 38, and Annemarie Schimmel's *And Muhammad Is His Messenger*, 11, 101.

pulp edition of the same ballad, penned by one Shaykh ʿAbd Allāh ibn Aḥmad (nicknamed il-ʿArabī). This edition is entitled *al-Jawāhir il-Bahīja fī Zawāj an-Nabī Ṣallā llāhu ʿAlayhi wa Sallam bi s-Sayyida Khadīja wa Dhikr Safarihi lish-Shām* (The delightful jewels about the marriage of the Prophet, peace and blessings of God be upon him, to the Lady Khadīja and an account of his journey to Syria)[13] and not only contains whole lines, which are absent in Littmann's edition, but also has some variations in wording. We will note the differences between the two versions whenever necessary.

This analysis is divided into three parts: chapter 5 gives a detailed account of the Prophet's trading journey to Syria and his marriage to Khadīja as described in the ballad; chapter 6 offers an analysis of the major themes in the ballad with the intention of examining the way in which the classical account of the Prophet's *sīra* (biography) is similar to or different from that of the folk treatment; and chapter 7 focuses on the literary texture of the narrative ballad and discusses both its colloquial diction and folk imagery.

13. Published in Ṭanṭā by Maktabat Ibrāhīm Muṣṭafā Tāj, n.d. Unless stated otherwise, each reference to Littmann's version of the ballad corresponds to that of Ibn Aḥmad. References are to Littmann's version because it is easily accessible to scholars.

CHAPTER 5

The Text

Littmann's version of the ballad consists of 222 stanzas that range from four to five lines with the exception of a few stanzas which consist of two or three lines. The majority of the ballad—143 stanzas—consists of five lines with the same rhyme scheme: *aaaba*. The rest of the stanzas commonly have four lines—with minor exceptions—with the rhyme scheme *aaba*.[1] Ibn Aḥmad's version of the ballad consists of 202 stanzas which range from five to twenty-one lines; the majority are five or nine lines and the rest are seven, eleven, or twenty-one lines. The ballad is composed in colloquial Egyptian Arabic, mainly in the Cairene dialect, but with a number of vocables in the *ṣaʿīdī* (Upper Egyptian dialect) whose presence is conspicuous. The folk literary form in which the ballad is cast is the *mawwāl*—a form believed to have originated in ninth-century Iraq during the reign of Hārūn ar-Rashīd. The *mawwāl* is often recited or sung to accompany a simple musical instrument called the *rabāba* (rebec, spike-fiddle) and relies on witty puns and wordplay.

In Egypt, the *mawwāl* is composed of two motifs (the terms here are far from being uniform for practitioners in the field apply them rather loosely): *al-akhḍar* (the green) which deals with the topics of love and the joy of life and *al-aḥmar* (the red; also known, especially in Upper Egypt, as the *wāw*) which deals with the pains of life, separation from the beloved, and complaints about the treachery of people and time. The Egyptian ballad relies heavily on paronomasia and is cast in the *basīṯ* meter. Traditionally the ballad has four *aqfāl* (lines) with the rhyme scheme: *aaaa*. But since it came to Egypt from Iraq, there are two known varieties: the five-line *mawwāl*, which is commonly called *al-khumāsī* or *al-aʿrag* (the lame), and the seven-line *mawwāl*, which is

1. Enno Littmann, *Mohammed Im Volksepos: Ein Neuarabisches Heilingenlied* (Copenhagen: Ejnar Munksgaard, 1950), 4.

called *as-subāᶜī, an-nuᶜmānī,* or *az-zuhērī.* The five-line ballad has the rhyme scheme: *aaaba;* the seven-line ballad has the rhyme scheme: *aaaaaba.* There are also other kinds of schemes such as *al-mardūf* (cumulative, incremental, or "ride pillion," according to Pierre Cachia), the *mughaṭṭā* (the concealed), and the *maftūḥ* (the open).[2]

The ballad forms part of the repertoire of the *madīḥ* (eulogy) sung in honor of the prophet Muḥammad.[3] The fact that the ballad has survived for over half a century, or maybe even longer, makes it all the more valuable for our search for the popular Muḥammad. The fact that it is authored by a literate shaykh does not necessarily mean that the ballad is not part of an oral literature. One should remember that the ballad is already part of the current repertoire in which, more often than not, authorship is neglected. One even has the suspicion that Ibn Aḥmad may have "recorded" an existing version of the ballad rather than composed it. There are more indications in Littmann's edition that point out the "orality" of the ballad.

The text of the ballad was dictated to Littmann by a Cairene by the name of Maḥmūd Ṣidqī, who collected it from an Upper Egyptian folksinger. Here is Ṣidqī's account of how the text was recorded:

Eulogy on the Story of the Prophet's Marriage to Khadīja and His Trading Journey with Her Goods and the Miracles He Performed During His Journey to Syria

In the Name of God the Most Compassionate the Most Merciful

I was one day sitting in front of my home on al-Malika Nazli Street near ᶜAbd al-Wahhāb Square at Giza when I heard a folk singer in his forties mention in his singing the story of the Prophet's—God's blessings be upon him—marriage to Khadīja and his trading journey with her goods to Syria. I called him, welcomed him in and said to him while smiling: "I would like you to dictate to me this *sīra* of the Prophet and I will reward you." He said: "With pleasure." I

2. See Kamal Abdel-Malek, *A Study of the Vernacular Poetry of Aḥmad Fuʾād Nigm* (Leiden: E. J. Brill, 1990), 89–90; Aḥmad Rushdī Ṣāliḥ, *Funūn al-Adab ash-Shaᶜbī,* vol. 1 (Cairo: Dār al-Fikr, 1956), 166–74; Pierre Cachia, *Popular Narrative Ballads of Modern Egypt* (Oxford: Oxford University Press, 1989) and "The Egyptian Mawwāl: Its Ancestry, Its Development, and Its Present Form," *Journal of Arabic Literature* 8 (1977), 77–103.

3. When Kamal Abdel-Malek recited the opening stanza to the Egyptian *maddāḥ* Shaykh ᶜAbd il-Fattāḥ il-ᶜIrasī, he recognized the ballad and ascertained that it was still part of the repertoire, although the last time he heard it sung was sometime in the 1960s. Abdel-Malek is currently writing a full-fledged study of the repertoire of Shaykh il-ᶜIrasī and many of his fellow *maddāḥīn.*

offered him cigarettes and coffee and he dictated to me the entire *sīra* in two sittings, Tuesday before noon and Wednesday morning. I asked him to sing the story again to make sure that the words were vocalised in accordance with his pronunciation. I found out that some portions were unwittingly left out by him. I proceeded to correct some words which were in his singing different from the way he had dictated. On God reliance is due—always.[4] (8)

The informant's comments on the discrepancies in the narrative between the different performances (or between the performance and the dictation provided by the folk-singer) and the different version of Ibn Aḥmad, demonstrate the orality and fluidity of the ballad. Internal evidence also confirms this oral quality—for instance, in stanza 1 the singer addresses the listener directly and urges him/her to pay attention and listen to the story of the ballad:

> Stand and listen to the story of the marriage of the beautiful one.
> (10)

Elsewhere the singer urges people to go on a pilgrimage to the Prophet's tomb, (16.18) or alerts the listeners to a shift in the narrative by addressing them through the epithet, *aṣḥāb l-afhām* (people of sound thinking or intelligence) (84.203). Is this orality, which seems to produce a different text with each performance, an example of the oral-formulaic theory of Lord and Parry?[5] Is there, then, no original text for this ballad, rather only a performance or a recitation? Is the performance also the act of creation? Are the author and the singer—or reciter—one and the same? The significance of these questions, however, cannot be lost on the folklorist.

The ballad starts with the traditional invocation of the Prophet's name and the expressed hope that the Prophet may intercede on behalf of the *maddāḥ* (eulogist) on the day of judgment. We are told that Muḥammad wants to settle down and marry. As would a contemporary Egyptian young man, Muḥammad duly consults his family about his marriage plans. Being an orphan, he goes to his uncle, Abū Ṭālib, to seek advice. Abū Ṭālib reacts favorably and promises to defray the

---

4. Parenthetical references are to Enno Littmann, *Mohammed Im Volksepos: Ein Neuarabisches Heilingenlied* (Copenhagen: Ejnar Munksgaard, 1950). The numbers refer to page numbers followed by stanza numbers.

5. See Albert Lord, *The Singer of Tales* (New York: Atheneum, 1965); Milman Parry, *The Making of Homeric Verse: The Collected Papers of Milman Parry*, ed. Adam Parry (Oxford, 1971).

wedding costs. Other uncles are duly notified: Ḥamza, al-ᶜAbbās and even the wicked Abū Lahab (described as the wealthiest uncle). Abū Lahab promises to pay for all the wedding costs only if Muḥammad is willing to go with him to show respect to the idols. With a pious admonition, Muḥammad chides Abū Lahab and refuses his conditions, vowing to earn the money needed by himself with the sweat of his brow and the labor of his right (i.e., pure) hand. Muḥammad is already called the Prophet—by the singer/narrator as well as the interlocutors in the ballad—even though he is reported in the classical accounts to have received the revelation only after his marriage to Khadīja.

One of Khadīja's slaves goes to tell her about Muḥammad. Khadīja falls in love with Muḥammad and sends for him, but, for a while, he demurs (being too timid to see her). They finally meet and he agrees to work for her by selling merchandise in Syria.

With a small trading caravan, that includes some of his uncles and even his opponent Abū Jahl, Muḥammad sets out for Syria. He is shown to have extraordinary physical strength: his strength surpasses even the strength of forty prophets, each of whom is endowed with the strength of forty men. He also performs a number of miracles. At his request, water gushes out of the scorched earth and date trees spring up instantly. During his journey, he meets many people to whom he preaches the message of Islam. Men, jinn, and even animals recognize him as the messenger of God. As in the *Sīra,* he is shown to preach Islam to the Christian monk Baḥīrā but, unlike in the *Sīra,* Muḥammad craftily disarms Baḥīrā in a conversation and even manages to convert him, along with his fellow monks, to Islam. Muḥammad also succeeds in fighting off the treachery of those who conspire to kill him. Abū Jahl, the *bête noire* of the *Sīra,* is constantly humbled and his conspiracies against Muḥammad thwarted. A wicked Jew and his one-eyed wife, who attempt to kill Muḥammad by throwing a rock on him from the roof of their house, are taught a severe lesson. The rock misses the divinely protected Prophet and kills the Jew's two children instead. Not only Muḥammad the prophet, but also Muḥammad the merchant is divinely guided. The angel Gabriel feeds him with precious "inside information" about the Syrian market. For instance the angel tells Muḥammad when it is more profitable to sell and when to hold off. To increase the value of the camels which Muḥammad sells, the angel causes the Syrian camels to lose their appetite and grow weak and emaciated. The panicky Syrian buyers rush to purchase Muḥammad's camels and other merchandise. In this way, Muḥammad manages to make a large profit; an item which is usually valued at 10 dirhems now sells for 1,000.

Back in Mecca, the anxious Khadīja receives Muḥammad with great joy. In passionate language, she expresses her burning love for him and proposes marriage. Once again, as would a dutiful Egyptian young man, Muḥammad goes to consult his uncles. One uncle objects that Khadīja is "a fickle girl" (74.171) but goes along with Muḥammad's desire to marry her anyway. The men agree to go to Khuwaylid, Khadīja's father, to ask for her hand. When the men arrive, they find Khuwaylid sitting in front of his house inebriated and holding a cup of wine in his hand. This is a significant detail that may be intended to prefigure the upcoming tension and conflict, since wine drinking is a taboo in Islam. Khuwaylid is shown to stand for Mecca's pagan values; values which run counter to Muḥammad and his message. As expected, Khuwaylid refuses Muḥammad's marriage proposal on the grounds that Muḥammad, being poor, is not an equal social match for Khadīja and her family. Tempers rise, and some of the uncles want to punish Khuwaylid for being arrogant and impertinent, but Muḥammad dissuades them.

On the way to Khadīja's house, Muḥammad leaves his uncles. A moving detail, designed to achieve pathos, is provided here. We are told that Muḥammad goes to lie down by his mother's grave. Muḥammad—the poor one, the orphan—now feels rejected and unwanted. What else can comfort him but the memory of the mother, whose affection and care he was deprived of ever since he was a toddler? This is perhaps the only time in the narrative when Muḥammad, otherwise the prophet triumphant *par excellence,* is shown to be vulnerable.

When al-ʿAbbās goes to fetch Muḥammad, he finds him asleep beside his mother's grave. He spots a snake crawling around the sleeping Muḥammad. Alarmed, al-ʿAbbās draws his *al-muhannadī* (Indian-made sword) to kill the snake, but the snake cries out to Muḥammad for help. The snake turns out to be one of the kings of the jinn. Muḥammad prevents al-ʿAbbās (wrongly called Muḥammad's cousin) from killing the jinn-turned-snake. Once saved, the snake thanks the Prophet and entreats him to intercede on its behalf on the day of judgment.

Another attempt is made to win Khuwaylid's consent for Khadīja's marriage to Muḥammad. In a patriarchal society—whether seventh-century Arabia or twentieth-century Egypt—a father's consent for his daughter's marriage has to be solicited, even though the daughter may be a forty-year-old widow reputed to be the wealthiest and most influential woman in town. Khadīja sends some of her attendants to her father to ask for his permission.

According to the Littmann version, Khuwaylid does not relent and insults the men Khadīja has sent—why Khadīja could not talk to her father directly is not explained. Muḥammad's uncles are now very angry. They scramble to beat Khuwaylid. Ḥamza draws on his Yemeni-made sword. Khuwaylid becomes frightened but laughs (nervously out of fear) and then runs away.

Here, as the narrative draws to an end, there is a sudden shift. Out of nowhere Abū Jahl, the pagan chief whose plots to kill Muḥammad have failed, springs onto the scene. He is seen chasing the accursed Khuwaylid while tears are streaming down his cheeks. This is rather puzzling: why does Abū Jahl chase Khuwaylid or weep so profusely? The answer to these confusing details can be found in the Ibn Aḥmad version. According to the Ibn Aḥmad version, Khadīja manages to obtain her father's consent for her marriage through the help of her "Uncle" Waraqa (Ibn Nawfal—he is in fact her cousin according to the classical sources). But the drunk father changes his mind once he becomes sober. He is seen at Khadīja's door objecting to her marriage to Muḥammad. Khadīja secretly slips nine hundred dinars in al-ʿAbbās's hands and requests that he give the money to her father as though it were a gift from Muḥammad's family. Khuwaylid accepts the money gladly and blesses the marriage. Meanwhile, driven by envy, Abū Jahl comes by to thwart Muḥammad's marriage plans. He rudely advises Muḥammad's uncles to marry him off to any of the women of the poor Arabs of Ghaṭfān, rather than to Khadīja, who is not his social match. The uncles are now very angry. They scramble to kill him; Abū Jahl becomes so frightened that he bursts out laughing nervously.

Both versions then show Abū Jahl stopping at one of the many Meccan idols. He looks at the idol with revulsion, then takes off his *naʿl* (shoes) with the intention of beating the idol—a supreme insult in Arab cultural symbolism. Iblīs, who is shown to take on the form of these idols, becomes very frightened of Abū Jahl and takes to flight. Abū Jahl continues to beat the idol, calling it "the most stinking fart" (90.219). Is Abū Jahl now recanting his pagan practices? Are the tears streaming down his cheeks tears of repentance? Is he about to embrace Islam? We are not directly told. The last we hear of Abū Jahl is that, after his sudden change of heart, he stays home for three days in utter dejection and confusion.

Echoing almost to the letter the typical end of Egyptian folk tales—where the hero marries his love and both *ʿāshu fi t-tabāt wi n-nabāt wi-khallifū ṣubyān wi banāt* (lived happily ever after and had boys and girls)—the ballad shows the Prophet as finally being able to marry Khadīja. Heaven and earth are bedecked for the occasion, and joy is present everywhere; even the *ḥūr* (beautiful maidens who are promised to pious Muslim men in paradise) are seen singing for the happy occasion.

CHAPTER 6

Text Analysis

The most striking feature about the narrative is its fluidity in terms of time and space. According to the classical biography *Sīrat Rasūl Allāh* by Ibn Isḥāq, Muḥammad received his call at the age of forty.[1] But in the present ballad, Muḥammad is already called *in-nabī* (the Prophet) even though he is presumed to be just a youth. He is shown to preach, perform miracles, and be recognized by men, jinn, and animals as the messenger of God.

Just as Muḥammad is made free of the bounds of time, so is he also not restricted by the bounds of space. When in Syria, for example, he disappears for an hour or so and manages to transfer himself to Mecca where he pays Khadīja a quick visit.[2]

Again, just as the bounds of time and space are not observed, so is the boundary between the natural and supernatural worlds also transcended. Throughout the ballad, divine intervention in the natural world is common. The angel Gabriel springs onto the scene so often that he becomes, in effect, one of the main characters—and at least once the devil himself shows up. Moreover, Muḥammad's many miracles, being in themselves a contravention of the natural order of things, appear to illustrate this point further.

Another striking feature about the narrative is the manifest xenophobia that permeates it. There are basically two groups at play in the ballad: the inside group, which is Muḥammad's own community (comprised of kinsmen, loyal slaves, companions, and Khadīja), and the

1. Ibn Isḥāq, *Sīrat Rasūl Allāh,* trans. A. Guillaume under the title, *The Life of Muhammad* (London: Oxford University Press, 1955).

2. On this miraculous act, see Enno Littmann, *Mohammed Im Volksepos: Ein Neuarabisches Heilingenlied* (Copenhagen: Ejnar Munksgaard, 1950), 56–62, stanzas 125–41.

outside group of non-Muslims (comprised of Christians, Jews, and pagans). There is tension between the two groups which is punctuated by frequent clashes. Throughout the narrative, negative epithets are given to non-Muslims. Abū Jahl and Khuwaylid, Khadīja's father, are each often called *il-malʿūn* (the accursed one) (24.38); Christians are accused of slyness (26.43); and a Jew is called a "dog and a scoundrel" (50.106).[3] One notices that negative epithets are sometimes made interchangeable among the non-Muslims. For example, a Jew is called a *kāfir* (infidel) and Abū Jahl, the pagan, is also called a *kāfir* and is described as far more sly than the Christians.[4]

The tension between the two groups continues until the outside group becomes totally absorbed by the inside group. By the end of the ballad, all non-Muslims are made to convert to Islam: Baḥīrā and his fellow monks, a Jew and his wife, Abū Jahl, and even some jinn. Notice that in the *Sīra,* Ibn Isḥāq does not mention Baḥīrā's conversion or Abū Jahl's; the latter is said to have remained Muḥammad's arch enemy until he was killed by Muḥammad's army at the battle of Badr.[5]

But nowhere else is the dichotomy between the inside and the outside groups made more manifest than in the case of Muḥammad's encounter with Baḥīrā, the famed monk. This dichotomy is subtly, but powerfully, described. When Muḥammad enters Baḥīrā's monastery, we are told that a *ṣanam* (idol), presumably a statue of Christ, falls and breaks—never to rise again *(ma-nʾām)* (42.83). In contrast, the people (the majority of whom are monks who are about to embrace Islam) rise up to greet the Prophet as a sign of respect for the one whose religion God himself set up—*ʾām* (42.84). At this point Baḥīrā's original destiny is effaced, and a new one replaces it. Here the Islam/Christianity dichotomy is depicted as a clash of destinies in which Islam is made to triumph and rule supreme.

An example of the details that are mentioned in passing in the *Sīra* is the necessity of consulting one's family and elders about major decisions. This detail is particularly stressed throughout the ballad. Muḥammad is shown as eager to consult his uncles—since he is an orphan—each time he needs to take a step of importance. The opening stanzas

3. Numbers in parentheses indicate page and stanza numbers from Littmann, *Mohammed Im Volksepos.*

4. A current Egyptian proverb which manifests Muslim suspicion of Christian Copts says: *ʾibṭī bala makr sagara (shagara) bala ṭarḥ* (A Copt who is without slyness is like a tree that does not bear fruit).

5. See *Encyclopaedia of Islam,* new edition (Leiden: E. J. Brill, 1960–), 868.

show Muḥammad expressing, to one of his uncles, his desire to settle down and marry and asking for his uncle's counsel and help. Muḥammad is also shown consulting his uncles about his journey to Syria and his marriage to Khadīja. The verb used for consulting is *shāwir*—a verb which is etymologically related to the oft-quoted Islamic term *shūrā* (consultative council). Before the journey to Syria, Khadīja says to Muḥammad:

> *ya-sīdī*[6] *shāwir iʿmāmak baʾa wi taʿāl*
> [O master, consult your uncles then come back].
>
> (20.26)

Muḥammad then goes to consult his uncles—an action which is reported in two separate and almost identical stanzas (29 and 161):

> After he had consulted his uncles, he returned.[7]

It is true in the *Sīra* that Muḥammad enlists his uncles' help to ask for Khadīja's hand. "The apostle of God," so the *Sīra* goes, "told his uncles of Khadīja's proposal, and his uncle Ḥamza b. ʿAbd al-Muṯṯalib went with him to Khuwaylid b. Asad and asked for her hand and he married her."[8] The difference is that the ballad puts an added stress on Muḥammad's frequent consultations with his uncles, even though it depicts him as a man of extraordinary powers who is especially favored by God. Muḥammad, in the ballad, may be shown to be above the strictures of the natural world (e.g., the bounds of time and space), but he is not above the world's social strictures. The ballad elaborates on the value of consultation and seeking advice partly by augmenting the scanty details given in the *Sīra* and partly by mentioning it several times. In so doing, the ballad seems to project native social values and perceptions on Muḥammad's life story.

Such projection can also be seen at work in certain details. Consider, for example, the curious detail about the wicked Abū Jahl that shows him filling up a well with earth so that neither Muḥammad, nor his followers in the trading caravan to Syria, may find water. The *Sīra* does

---

6. "*Yā-sīdī*" in colloquial Egyptian Arabic may also be used as a familiar way of addressing a friend.

7. Stanza 161 (p. 70), is slightly different: "*min baʿd ma-shāwir ʿalā* [sic] *ʿammu rigiʿ tānī*" (After he had consulted his uncle, he returned). *ʿAlā* is obviously a mistake since it changes the meaning to "after he had pointed his uncle out."

8. Ibn Isḥāq, *Sīrat*, 82.

not mention Abū Jahl's wicked deed or even that he went to Syria with Muḥammad's caravan. But the *Sīra* does mention that during the battle of Badr, Muḥammad ordered that some wells be dried up in order to deprive his enemies—such as Abū Jahl—of water.[9] What does this transposition mean? Does the ballad deem the act of filling up a well with earth, when water is such a precious commodity in the desert, too cruel for the kind Prophet, but cruel enough to be expected of the wicked Abū Jahl?

A more subtle example of transposition may be seen in the way in which the prophet Muḥammad is made, at times, to appear Christ-like. Consider Muḥammad's words to the Jew who recants his Judaism and embraces Islam:

> Observe faithfully the prayer and the Prophet's ways
> And tomorrow you will be with us in the most spacious Paradise.
> (56.121)

These words are almost, verbatim, the same words Christ used when speaking to one of the recanting robbers who was crucified with him: "And He [Christ] said to him [the robber], 'Truly I say to you, today you shall be with Me in Paradise' " (Luke 23:43).

There is also something Christ-like about the miracles attributed to Muḥammad in the ballad. The Bible mentions that Christ, for example, healed a paralytic: "I say to you, rise, take up your pallet and go home" (Mark 2:11). Curiously, the ballad reports that Muḥammad also healed a *siṭīḥa* (paralytic in the Egyptian vernacular) (24.39). Like Christ, Muḥammad heals the blind and feeds a multitude—although Muḥammad feeds the people by causing the date pits he throws out to grow up instantly into date trees, not by splitting loaves and fish. His miracles are also not only evidentiary but functional: by healing and feeding people these miracles serve a definite purpose and satisfy a real need.

Admittedly, the examples just cited can be regarded as pious attempts by the unknown author, or authors, to attribute supernatural powers to Muḥammad, who is held as unique both among ordinary men as well as among prophets. This may be true if one looks at these miracles separately, but indeed one cannot escape the impression that a Christ-like image is projected onto Muḥammad. Even if this projection is true, what does it mean? One can only speculate that it may be a sign of a rather defensive streak in the narrative. The ballad may be

9. See *Encyclopaedia of Islam*, new edition, 868.

reacting to Christian criticisms that, unlike Christ, Muḥammad is not known to have performed evidentiary miracles, and that, therefore, his credibility as a true prophet is in question. By attributing miracles to Muḥammad that are as great as those of Christ, the ballad attempts to counter the charges levelled at the Prophet by Christians.

Another intriguing example of projection is the similarity between Abū Jahl, as portrayed in the *Sīra,* and a wicked Jew, who is mentioned in the ballad but not in the *Sīra.* In the *Sīra* we are told that Abū Jahl once tried to kill Muḥammad by dropping a big rock on him.[10] The ballad also mentions that Abū Jahl conspires to kill Muḥammad, but it does not mention the rock-dropping incident. Rather, the ballad attributes this incident to a Jew and his one-eyed wife—who later recant and embrace Islam. This latter version of the ballad is not even mentioned in the *Sīra.* Both the Jew and Abū Jahl are called *kāfir* (infidel) in the ballad and perhaps the interchangeability of their wicked deeds and the condemning epithets between the two evil-doers suggests a common negative attitude towards all non-Muslims depicted as "the other" in the ballad. This "us-versus-them" dichotomy seems to underline the Islamic perception that whatever lies beyond the abode of Islam belongs to the abode of war and that *"al-kufr milla wāḥida"* (unbelief is one nation).

Thus far we have seen the way in which the folk ballad treats the story of Muḥammad's life and the manner in which it creates its own account; an account which does not always tally with the classical or official *Sīra.* However, one should not assume that the *Sīra* and folk ballad totally contradict each other. Indeed, there is more here than meets the eye. Some subterranean links between the official and popular tradition can be found only if one is willing to dig below the surface.

A closer look at the ballad will show that, although its text and texture clearly reveal its folk source, some of its motifs echo the classical lore. Throughout the ballad, a two-pronged *leitmotif* is discernable: first, the Prophet's noble qualities and outward beauty and second, the proofs of his prophethood. Repeatedly the Prophet is described as the exemplar of human beauty and as a true miracle-making prophet often acknowledged by others as God's messenger. Does this two-pronged *leitmotif* not echo the classical genres known as *shamāʾil* (which extolls the Prophet's lofty moral qualities and physical beauty) and *dalāʾil* (which recounts the proofs of Muḥammad's prophethood)? Let us trace this notion a bit further.

10. Ibn Isḥāq, *Sīrat,* 135.

The two genres probably came into being sometime in the tenth century. Their earliest known authors were Abū Nuᶜaym al-Iṣfahānī (d. 1037), a mystic and historian, and al-Bayhaqī (d. 1066).

Both [works] are more or less biographies of the Prophet, studded with evidentiary miracles—those that happened before and after his call to prophethood and those that pointed to his exalted status as the last Prophet. Both sources speak of his noble genealogy and his qualities and indulge in telling many of the miracles through which man and animals recognized him as God's special messenger. Such tales formed the bases for legends and poems in which popular views about Muhammad were to be reflected throughout the centuries.[11]

Quoting ᶜAlī, the Prophet's cousin and son-in-law, Abū ᶜĪsā at-Tirmidhī gives us the earliest account of the Prophet's physical attributes in the first basic book of the *shamāʾil* genre:

Muhammad was middle-sized, did not have lank or crisp hair, was not fat, had a white circular face, wide black eyes, and long eye-lashes. When he walked, he walked as though he went down a declivity. He had the "seal of prophecy" between his shoulder blades. . . . He was bulky. His face shone like the moon. He was taller than middling stature but shorter than conspicuous tallness. He had thick, curly hair. The plaits of his hair were parted. His hair reached beyond the lobe of his ear. His complexion was *azhar* [bright, luminous]. Muhammad had a wide forehead, and fine, long, arched eyebrows which did not meet. Between his eyebrows there was a vein that distended when he was angry. The upper part of his nose was hooked; he was thick bearded, had smooth cheeks, a strong mouth, and his teeth were set apart. He had thin hair on his chest. His neck was like the neck of an ivory statue, with the purity of silver. Muhammad was proportionate, stout, firm-gripped, even of belly and chest broad-chested and broad-shouldered.[12]

Now, let us analyze how these two classical genres are echoed in this narrative ballad. The ballad is full of supreme praise for the Prophet. His physical beauty is unsurpassed and his moral character is unblemished. His physical beauty is reflected in his character and vice versa. In the ballad, the Prophet is called *kaḥīl al-ᶜēn* (he who has kohl-colored eyes). In fact the mention of such a quality recurs many times

11. Annemarie Schimmel, *And Muhammad Is His Messenger* (Chapel Hill: University of North Carolina Press, 1985), 33.
12. Ibid., 34.

and becomes an inseparable epithet of the Prophet. The ballad opens with this description as well as with the use of the word *zēn* (the beautiful one):

> *yā ʾalbī ṣallī ʿlā kaḥīl al-ʿen*
> *yōm il-ʾiyāma ykunlak fī sh-shadāyid ʿēn*
> *min baʿd-i madḥ-i n-nabī w ahlu l-kirām yā zēn*
> *ʾuʾaf w istimiʿ dī l-ḥikāya f(ī) gawāz iz-zēn*
> [My heart, pray for the one with the kohl-coloured eyes
> On the Last Day, he will support you against the horrors
> After praising the Prophet and his noble family, O beautiful one,
> Stand and listen to the story of the marriage of the beautiful one].[13]
> (10.1)

The Prophet is also called *malīḥ al-wagh* (the one with a beautiful face) (18.25), *kāmil il-awṣāf* (the one who possesses perfect qualities) (70.160), and *kāmil il-hindām* (the well-groomed one) (72.168). Elsewhere the Prophet is shown to have a lovely fragrance that permeates the places he frequents.

This fascination with the Prophet's physical beauty can also be seen in the *shamāʾil* and *dalāʾil* literature. Likewise, Abū Nuʿaym tells us about the Prophet's lovely fragrance. Muḥammad's perspiration is claimed to have been collected and used as perfume by some women who were close to him. Moreover, the Prophet's face is described as beautiful *(maliḥ)* and his hands are described as "cooler than ice and softer than silk."[14]

As in the *Sīra*, the *shamāʾil*, and the *dalāʾil* literature, the ballad stresses the Prophet's noble genealogy. He is called *aṣīl il-gadd* (the one who has noble ancestry) (16.16), *sayyid walad ʿadnān* (the lord of the tribe of ʿAdnān) (32.60), *il-muṣṭafā l-ʿadnān* (the ʿAdnāni chosen one), and *ṣafwit id-dayyān* (the cream of God's creation) (32.62). Descent from ʿAdnān, the legendary ancestor of pure Arabs, is meant to confer particular honor on the Prophet. This idea of noble genealogy—where the person is shown to have a known line of descent that links him/her to a great ancestor—might have a strong appeal to Egypt's labor class who follow a naming system which does not preserve one's family name. This makes any attempt to trace one's descent beyond one's grandfather a difficult, if not at times, impossible task.

---

13. In Ibn Aḥmad's version the first line reads: *"yā-ʾalbī ṣallī ʿlā l-hādī kaḥīl al-ʿēn."* The last line has the standard *zawāg* instead of the colloquial *gawāz*.

14. Schimmel, *And Muhammad Is His Messenger*, 34.

Echoing the *Sīra,* the ballad also dwells on Muḥammad's light. His visage beams wherever he goes; he is now described as a full moon (60.132), now as more brilliant than the sun itself (46.95). Whenever he enters Khadīja's house, lights shine forth from him *(faggit il-anwār)* (18.22); he is resplendent *(bahiyy in-nūr)* (20.27); and his forehead shines in the dark *(gibīnak fī ẓ-ẓalām shāliᶜ)* (28.53). Such a preoccupation with the Prophet's light may also suggest possible Ṣūfī influences, especially when we also consider the mystic language which describes the love for the Prophet. Muḥammad's light is shown to dazzle and captivate people:

> Muḥammad who spellbinds lovers with his beauty
> His beaming face, his perfect wits.
>
> (191.185)

He is called by Baḥīrā: *"ghāyit il-maṭlūb"* (the goal of what is sought) (44.93) and *"yā ḥabībī yā ḥa''"* (my beloved the true one) (44.90). For Baḥīrā, love for the Prophet sets the heart ablaze, grinds the body, and takes away the mind (38.74).

But stronger evidence of Ṣūfī influences can be seen in the images that describe *"nūr muḥammad"* [15] not only as captivating lovers, but also as shining forth around the cosmos. As Muḥammad enters the neighborhood where Khadīja lives, she sees his beauty illuminating the cosmos (56.125). Elsewhere, Muḥammad's light shines over the planets (30.57). These images and others are unmistakably Ṣūfī influenced.

The physical and spiritual *shamā'il* of the Prophet are paraded throughout the ballad. He is seen as superior to all people and prophets—not only in his spiritual powers but in his physical powers as well. This can be seen in the ballad when Muḥammad carries, with his bare hands, heavy loads of goods that would normally require many men to carry. God favors him with unmatched physical strength:

> God, Lord of the people, the One, the Forgiver
> Assuredly, gave each one of the chosen prophets
> The strength of forty men
> But our Prophet was given the strength of forty prophets
> Multiply 40 × 40, see how strong the Chosen One is.
>
> (22.33)

---

15. On the light of Muḥammad, see Tor Andrae, *Die Person Muhammeds in Lehre und Glauben seiner Gemeinde* (Stockholm: P. A. Vorstedt og soner, 1918), 319ff. Schimmel, *And Muhammad Is His Messenger,* 123–43.

The Prophet's superior physical qualities are not differentiated from his spiritual ones. In fact both qualities are seen to integrate and blend harmoniously. As the exalted spiritual guide, Muḥammad is not seen as oblivious to the concerns or joys of the physical world. The ballad shows him as a merchant preoccupied by the prospects of material gains and losses. He savors the gifts—a silk garment and jewel-studded chair—which Khadīja gives him. He is also shown to be responsive to Khadīja's beauty and coquetry. In his dealings with Khadīja, Muḥammad's spiritual and physical qualities are invoked. She is shown to be attracted to him both as a strong and handsome man, and as a unique prophet who is favored by God. Stanzas that describe the love between Khadīja and Muḥammad evoke both the spiritual and the physical. Consider this stanza which describes Abū Bakr's dream about Muḥammad and Khadīja. Abū Bakr says to Ḥamza, the Prophet's uncle:

> He told him I saw the moon hovering in the midst of Mecca
> It rose to Heaven with ever-increasing light,
> Repeatedly coming down with ever-increasing light.
> It stepped down and entered Khadīja's home in joy
> Then clung to her bosom from under her loin-cloth.
>
> (80.188)

The moon, which is a standard symbol of beauty in Egyptian folklore, represents Muḥammad. In a highly suggestive dream language, the moon is in an excitable state—hovering around, going up and down with an ever-increasing pace. Then there is entering and clinging to the areas of the human body that are normally covered. Images of Muḥammad, the spiritual guide, and Muḥammad, the passionate lover who clings to Khadīja's bare body, are powerfully and erotically blended.

Elsewhere Khadīja flirtatiously tells Muḥammad of her love for him. Meaning herself, but speaking in the third person, she explains the effects of her love for Muḥammad:

> *ṣabbaḥtahā min gharāmak lazmit il-awrād*
> [Her love for you obliges her to recite portions of the Qurʾān in the morning].
>
> (72.165)

There are two key words here: *ṣabbaḥtahā* (you make her get up in the morning) and *lazmit* (obliged). Provided one is ritually clean, reading the Qur'ān can be done anytime. So, why is it an obligation to be performed immediately after getting up in the morning? These lines seem to conjure up the image of a love-stricken woman who wakes up from, perhaps, an erotic dream and seeks to exorcise her thoughts by reading portions of the Qur'ān. Here the folk imagination eroticizes the love for the beautiful Prophet and then transforms the spiritual and the abstract into the physical and the graspable.

CHAPTER 7

The Texture

The colloquial diction of the ballad gives a strong oral quality to the text—as does the imagery and the particular literary devices characteristic of the *mawwāl* form. The ballad abounds with examples of paronomasia. As is characteristic of the *mawwāl,* paronomasia is achieved in basically two ways: either by using the same word in two or more different meanings (e.g., well as in to do something well and a well of water) or by using two false cognates (e.g., well and we'll or we will). In the ballad, however, paronomasia goes beyond mere word-play and adds more depth to its literary texture. Notice, for instance, the way the word *ʿēn* is utilized. In stanza 1 it is used as a pun:

> *yāʾ albī ṣallī ʿalā kaḥīl al-ʿēn*
> *yōm il-ʾiyāma ykūnlak fī sh-shadāyid ʿēn*
> [My heart, pray for the one with the kohl-colored eyes
> On the Last Day, he will support you against the horrors].[1]
>
> (10.1)

ʿĒn in the first line means "eye" and in the second means "support." *ʿĒn* is used rather curiously as the equivalent of heart, as in this line:

> *wi l-ḥūr ghannit wi ʾālit ifraḥī yā ʿēn*
> [Houris sang and said: Rejoice o heart (o eye)].
>
> (92.221)

1. Numbers in parentheses indicate page and stanza numbers from Enno Littmann, *Mohammed Im Volksepos: Ein Neuarabisches Heilingenlied* (Copenhagen: Ejnar Munksgaard, 1950).

Elsewhere *ʿēn* is made to stand for both sight and insight. The Jewish woman who, along with her husband, plots to kill Muḥammad by dropping a rock on him from the roof of their home is described as *ʿēnhā ʿōra* (one-eyed). She is wicked and an infidel. Her spiritual handicap is projected somatically. She is half-blind both literally and figuratively. We are told that the prophet's radiance restores sight to her blind eye a moment or so before she drops the rock. She misses the Prophet and instead unwittingly kills her two children.

Cognates can also be used as antonyms. The word *baṭṭāl,* which can mean "a scoundrel" as well as "invalid, null, and void," is at one point contrasted with the word *baṭal* (hero). The two words are derived from the same root: BṬL. Madkūr, one of Khadīja's slaves, is called *Baṭal* (84.202) but the wicked Jew is called *baṭṭāl* (50.106). Other examples include words like *zād* (26.43; 72.165) meaning "food" and "increased"; *nār* (42.85) meaning "fire" and "lit"; *aḥlāmu* meaning "his dreams"; and the distorted *ʾaḥlā-mu* (64.144) meaning "more sweet than he."

Personal names are used as adjectival epithets. Consider the names of slaves: Mufliḥ (the successful one), Maysara (easiness), and Nagāḥ (success). Madkūr—who is called Baṭal (hero)—is derived from the root *dakar* (*dhakar* in classical Arabic; in general /dh/ becomes /d/ in colloquial Egyptian Arabic) meaning male. This name conjures up the notion of strength or virility in the Egyptian social idiom.

Throughout the ballad, the level of the diction varies from the purely colloquial to the conspicuously classical and from the terse to the effete. By and large the Prophet's speech is in literary Arabic—both grammatical and proper. His speech is clearly different from the speech of other characters in the ballad. For example, the Prophet uses highly formulaic language that expresses Islamic piety. God is often referred to as *ʾādir* (powerful) (14.10), *lā ilāha siwāh* (there is no god but He) (14.10), *rabb-i l-bayt* (the lord of the sanctuary) (14.11), *il-ḥaʾʾ* (Truth) (44.90; 76.181), and *wāḥid aḥad* (the one and only) (12.8). At times the notions Muḥammad expresses are conspicuously complex and philosophical, and the diction is made to correspond accordingly. This creates some tension in the otherwise smooth narrative. Consider, for example, the Prophet's speech to Abū Lahab when the latter asks him to show respect to the Meccan idols:

> *allāh wāḥid aḥad mā-lu rafīʾ wi anīs*
> *wa lā shabīh yishbihu khālī ʿan il-a ʿrāḍ*
> [God the one and the only has no associate or companion
> No one resembles him; He is free from accidents].
>
> (12.8)

The last line contains highly philosophical ideas about God being pure essence and devoid of all accidents. With the use of the rather unfamiliar preposition *ʿan* in *khālī ʿan* (more commonly *khālī min*) the line sounds like the kind of sentence one may come across in a philosophical work on God. Elsewhere the Prophet is made to say about God:

> And he formed (His) servant a human being after (the servant) had been nothing.
>
> (14.10)

Does this image not echo the philosophical notion that describes the active intellect which causes something to pass from the potential to the actual state? What is the origin of these philosophical notions in the ballad? Does this give evidence of a folk awareness of philosophical subjects—an awareness which was thought to have been the exclusive pride of the educated elite? Or is this the work of an educated editing hand—such as Shaykh Ibn Aḥmad's—that may have at one point tampered with the folk narrative? If indeed that were the case, one would have expected to find Littmann's version of the ballad—which is presumed to be an authorless, orally transmitted piece—free from such philosophical notions. Or could it be the influence of learned Ṣūfī concepts which are known to the folk *maddāḥīn* and their mostly unlettered audience? We must admit that this is rather puzzling.

One also notices a mixture of regional dialects in the ballad. The colloquial interrogative *ēsh,* which is used several times, may sound like Levantine Arabic; contemporary Egyptians use *ēh* instead. However, *ēsh* along with *ēh* was definitely used in Egypt in the last century and perhaps even at the turn of the century as Spiro's dictionary of Egyptian Arabic indicates.[2] There is also evidence of some *ṣaʿīdī* (Upper Egyptian) dialect, as seen in this line from Ibn Aḥmad's version:

> *hayyā sʿifū lī walīma dilwakīt fī l-ḥāl*
> [Come, hurry up, and make me a banquet immediately].

Dilwakīt is definitely *ṣaʿīdī* for "right now, immediately," which in the Cairene dialect would be *dilwaʾtī.* Ibn Aḥmad cites *dilwakīt* whereas Littmann uses a synonymous Cairene phrase, *bi l-ʿagal* (38.74). Other examples include *ḥadāh* (chez-lui) (56.124) instead of the Cairene *ʿandu;*

2. Socrates Spiro, *An Arabic-English Dictionary of the Colloquial Arabic of Egypt* (Beirut: Maktabat Lubnān, 1973), 26.

and *ʿād*[3] (totally) (58.130) instead of *kull*. The *ṣaʿīdī* dialect and pronunciation, however, are not always maintained and seem to be haphazardly used. This may be attributed to the fact that Littmann's informant was a Cairene whereas the singer of the ballad was a *ṣaʿīdī*. In fact, we are told by Littmann that his informant transmitted the text of the ballad in a Cairene pronunciation where the *ṣaʿīdī* hard "g" was sometimes given as a Cairene "ʾ" (5).

There is also a mixture of linguistic levels. Both literary and colloquial Arabic are employed. Unlike other characters in the ballad, the Prophet is made to speak mostly in literary Arabic rather than in the colloquial. This should not be surprising, because Muhammad's speech is supposed to set him apart from the rest. As he is shown to be superior in other qualities, likewise he is superior in his speech. The implication here is that the literary Arabic is superior to the colloquial Arabic with the latter being routinely dismissed as a linguistic degeneration of the former. Islam's formal lore is exclusively in the classical literary Arabic: the Qurʾān, the *ḥadīth*, and all the works on theology and law. Moreover, the Qurʾān's uniqueness lies in the linguistic excellence of its classical literary Arabic. In addition to all of these reasons that help classical Arabic maintain its supremacy, there is also the important factor that all the religious duties that a Muslim—especially an Arab Muslim—has to perform must be carried out in classical Arabic. Take the daily ritual prayer, for example. This prayer is a fixed formula which is spoken exclusively in literary Arabic. A Muslim repeats this formula daily, and cannot improvise or pray directly to God in a native language nor in an Arabic colloquial tongue. Likewise, the Islamic *shahāda* (testimony of faith): *ashhadu allā ilāha illā llāh wa-anna Muḥammadan rasūlu llāh* (I bear witness that there is no god but God and Muḥammad is His messenger) is a fixed phrase formula. One cannot imagine an Egyptian Muslim expressing the first part of the testimony in the colloquial by saying for example, *mafīsh ilāh illā rabbinā* (a close English equivalent is "there ain't no god except God").

In fact the colloquial is often dismissed as unfit to express Islamic piety, and to use it, for this or a similar purpose, would be—in the words of an Egyptian author—tantamount to a preposterous act of *ilḥād lughawī* (linguistic heresy).[4] That is why, unlike ordinary men, the Prophet has to speak in literary Arabic. Status here is illustrated

---

3. Ibn Aḥmad does not have "*ʿād*."

4. ʿAbbās Ḥasan, *"al-Daʿwa ilā l-ʿĀmmiyya wa Tark al-Iʿrāb Intikās fī l-Jahāla wa Jināya ʿalā l-Qawmiyya,"* *Risālat al-Islām* 9 (1957), 149.

through the use of different levels of language. Literary Arabic with its inflections and terse structures is believed, even by the unlettered folk, to be superior to the colloquial, and has, therefore, been chosen as the idiom for the sublime utterances of the beloved Prophet.

This Egyptian popular narrative ballad is both a literary work of high merit and an example of Egyptian Muslim veneration of the prophet Muḥammad. The narrative projects—much like Ibn Isḥāq's classical biography of the Prophet—the fundamental worldview of the prophet Muḥammad's absolute superiority over all other prophets (let alone other men). However the Egyptian ballad has some special features: (1) fluidity in terms of time and space: Muḥammad is shown to perform miracles all the time, and be recognized by men, jinn, animals, and even inanimate things as the true messenger of God; (2) manifest xenophobia: all non-Muslims are given negative, and at times interchangeable, epithets. The tension between the Muslims and the non-Muslims is eliminated only when the latter are totally absorbed into the community of the Muslims through conversion to Islam—even the famous Christian monk Baḥīrā converts; (3) projecting a Christ-like image on Muḥammad; (4) a linguistic code is made to correspond to status: the Prophet's superiority is underlined by making his speech in terse classical Arabic while the characters inferior to him are made to speak mostly in colloquial Egyptian Arabic.

Epilogue

After reading the previous chapters on popular poetry in honor of the prophet Muḥammad, the reader will doubtless have noticed the poets' skill in expressing their feelings, as well as those feelings shared by the community of believers, in a style that conforms completely to the literary and/or oral traditions of their respective cultures. For a nontutored reader who encounters poetry in honor of the Prophet for the first time, following the comparatively logical development of the story of the Prophet's wedding (in the Egyptian folk ballad) may be easier than disentangling the complicated web of allusions in the poems from the Indo-Muslim tradition.

One reason this may seem easier is that the Egyptian bard has described an actual historical event—decorated, of course, with romantic and hagiographic flourishes. Yet even in this ballad, one feels something that seems typical of the simplest religious poetry in Islamic lands. We refer here to the ease with which an unknown author, or perhaps singer, applies the terminology of traditional Islam and, at times, Ṣūfī thought to a historical topic. It is remarkable how in both the Arabic and Indian traditions the theological vocabulary of classical Islam forms a substantial part of the tradition even on the so-called folk-level. The coexistence of both classical and colloquial Arabic in the Egyptian ballad and Hindi-Urdu in their Sanskritized and Perso-Arabicized forms (in Muḥsin Kākorawī's panegyric) is a powerful testimony to the blurring of boundaries in the devotional tradition. Similar observations could be made for popular Turkish religious songs and, basically, for the entire vocabulary used by the elder generation. The mixture of lively narrative and inherited expressions and images constitutes the peculiar charm of the Egyptian rendering of the Prophet's wedding.

Understandably, the influence of the classical language is much more visible in the convoluted style of Muḥsin Kākorawī's grand *qaṣīda* in honor of the Prophet—a poem that offers considerable difficulties to readers, listeners, and especially translators. Muḥsin Kākorawī was a typical representative of the *sabk-i hindī*—the "Indian style" of Persian poetry which deeply influenced the emerging Urdu poetry in the eighteenth and nineteenth centuries. (Ghālib's *qaṣīda* in honor of the Prophet, written in 1828, is an excellent example of the application of this style to Persian.) The combination of lofty philosophical terms with the unexpected turns to idiomatic everyday language is one of the characteristics of this *sabk-i hindī*.

It is interesting to note that this grand Urdu *qaṣīda*, for which Muḥsin Kākorawī is famed, can also be viewed from a different perspective. Since the poem rhymes in the letter "l" ("*lām*" in Arabic), it is a *lāmiyya* (an l-rhyming poem). In the literary history of the Arab world there are two famous examples of this genre: one is the *Lāmiyyat al-ʿArab*, or the Arabian *lāmiyya*, ascribed to the pre-Islamic poet Shanfarā, whose description of his journey through the desert is of unusual power; the second is the famous *Lāmiyyat al-ʿAjam*, or the Persian *lāmiyya*, by the Persian-born author Tughrāʾī—a long Arabic poem composed in Baghdad in about 1112. Thus Kākorawī's use of the rhyme scheme calls to mind these famous works, and perhaps he thought of his panegyric as the *Lāmiyyat al-Hind*—the Indian variant of this form.

The ways in which the author blends Indian and Muslim themes is highly interesting. One knows how important the theme of the cloud is in Muslim poetical language as it reminds the reader, in religious contexts, of the "cloud of mercy." However, this idea is not only found in the Muslim world, it is well known in other cultures of the East as well. Thus, in the *Saddhamapundarika*, a widely studied Buddhist work, the Buddha appears as a large rain cloud which blesses the world. In Muslim Sindhi literature, the liveliest description of the arriving clouds is contained in the *wāʾī* of Shāh ʿAbdul Laṭīf's *Sūr Sārang*. In this poem the Prophet is the longed-for rain cloud who is asked to bless the whole world (especially the province of Sind) and in doing so revives the dead hearts of all those who need his help. In classical Indian literature, the combination of the monsoon clouds with the theme of the *virahinī* (the longing young woman) is traditional; while classical Persian poetry of the eleventh and twelfth centuries boasts of powerful descriptions of clouds which appear in the sky like huge black elephants. In the Sindhi tradition, the poet could sometimes interpret the red lightning bolts as manifestations of the spiritual bridegroom—the "Prince of Medina"—who, traditionally, is attired in red. One can also extend the cloud imagery to another aspect of the Muḥammad legend: according to tradition, whenever he walked a small cloud appeared over his head to protect him from the scorching sun. Allusions to this story are still found in the Islamic world.

Although the cloud seems to constitute a common denominator for Hindu and Muslim poetry, the combination of material from both traditions in Kākorawī's poem is quite astounding for readers without experience in the often syncretistic character of Indo-Muslim literature. As the reaction to these poems shows, the mixture was not easy for some more orthodox believers to accept. Yet, thanks to the two linguistic levels—the Hindi and the Perso-Arabic—the two traditions are neatly distinguished.

As difficult as it must have been for traditional Muslims to enjoy the lilting Hindi verses of the *qaṣīda*'s introduction with their allusions to Indian and Hindu literary motifs, uninitiated readers found it equally difficult to struggle through the highly technical language of Islamic theology which the poet uses in the second part. The *qaṣīda*'s first two parts seem almost incompatible in their use of language, idiom, and symbols, but in the final section the tension is resolved at a sweet, convincing linguistic level in the expression of hope that the poet would be forgiven at judgment day thanks to his skillful eulogy for the beloved Prophet—a hope which Muslim poets have traditionally uttered at the end of their poems—in Arabic, Persian, Turkish, Swahili, or any of the Indian languages. In Kākorawī's *qaṣīda,* the idea expressed in the concluding verses (i.e., that Gabriel invites the poet to recite his verse in the presence of the heavenly gathering) is delightful, and the closing line also shows the poet's grasp of traditional rhetorical devices, as the "return to the beginning" was considered highly elegant.

Of a totally different ethos are the Sindhi *maulūds* by ʿAbd ur-Raʾūf Bhaṭṭī. What are we to make of these? Here we encounter a real bridal mysticism well known in the medieval Christian world as an interpretation of the Song of Solomon. The Indian *virahinī* tradition, taken over into Muslim popular poetry, is directed here toward the Prophet. Although classical Islam has seen him as a father figure, role model, or intensely beloved and venerated friend, finding him depicted as "bridegroom of the soul" in any but Indo-Muslim literature would be difficult. To be sure, poets in other parts of the Muslim world have not hesitated to devote poems to his marriage with Khadīja—as becomes so clear from the Egyptian ballad analyzed in this context (there also exists at least one Turkish ballad about the Prophet's marriage). However, his marriages with the wives he wed after Khadīja's death have never inspired any poetry: the great Khadīja *(khadīja al-kubrā)* remained an ideal that was equally dear to Sunni and Shīʿī Muslims. Yet, despite an interest in a very earthly event, such as his marriage to Khadīja, it seems quite unusual that one should portray deep affection and love for the Prophet through the metaphor of a longing bride for her future husband. The idea is surprising and may even be shocking for the reader who is unaware of the Sindhi-Panjabi tradition.

Still, one may find some possible antecedent in the Islamic literature of earlier centuries: was not Zulaykhā, Potiphar's wife, infatuated with Yūsuf (Joseph), who like Muḥammad was a God-sent prophet? For poets in the classical tradition, this infatuation (which is attested in *Sūra* 12 of the Qurʾān) serves as a model of their longing for the divine beloved. The attempts of the longing woman, her resignation, and—not according to the Qurʾān but according to legend and tradition—her final marriage to Yūsuf, could be seen as symbols for the development of the soul, from *nafs ammāra* (the soul that incites to evil) (*Sūra* 12:53) to concupiscence, through suffering into the *nafs muṭmaʾinna* (the soul at peace) (*Sūra* 89:27). Yūsuf, the manifestation of that divine beauty which by necessity evokes love, is, like all the prophets, a forerunner of Muḥammad, the final prophet. His beauty, as mystics believe, is only part of the radiant beauty of the last messenger, Muḥammad. In the application of the motif of yearning, love, and final marriage to the prophet Muḥammad, some echoes of the love story of Yūsuf and Zulaykhā may have played a role. The Qurʾānic tradition was, as is often the case in Sindhi, merged with the love stories of the heroines of the Indus Valley. In this connection one should remember that the first Indo-Persian *mathnawīs* (epic narratives) devoted to the tragic Sindhi love story of *Sassui-Puṅhuṅ* in the early seventeenth century were modeled on Jāmī's (d. 1492) great epic poem *Yūsuf-Zulaykhā*.

Whatever the reason for the symbolism may be, ʿAbd ur-Raʾūf Bhaṭṭī's poems are wonderful examples of the very personal relations between the believer and the Prophet (and the Western reader will be strangely reminded of the love songs of medieval German nuns who experienced a similar "love affair" with Jesus and expressed their longing in a language that is quite realistic in its description of the bridal bed, kissing, and denudation). However, Bhaṭṭī's verses not only express an intense love for the Prophet, they also offer enjoyable insights into popular customs connected with the wedding ceremonies in a Sindhi village. The transformation of the beloved Prince Puṅhuṅ (the Baloch) into the "Hashimite bridegroom" is a truly fascinating example of indigenization.

Can the use of the *virahinī* motif in this devotional poetry, with its nuances of the Yūsuf-Zulaykhā tradition and its associated bridal symbolism, hold any other significance? It could, of course, be interpreted as a popularization of the mystical teachings concerning the final unification of the human soul with the *ḥaqīqa al-muḥammadiyya* (the Muḥammadan reality). According to theories developed in the Ṣūfī orders under the influence of Ibn ʿArabī's (d. 1240) teachings, this spiritual stage can be reached after wandering through the stations of the prophets who preceded Muḥammad. One finds such speculations in the poetry and prose of Bhaṭṭī's famous contemporary in Delhi, Khwāja Mīr Dard (d. 1785), whose descriptions of his unification with the *ḥaqīqa al-muḥammadiyya* (as given in the *ʿIlm ul-Kitāb*) are quite abstract and technical. Yet, even this great mystical writer, in the urban tradition of the Delhi Naqshbandiyya, was aware of the imagery of the female soul. In the work of his father (Nāṣir Muḥammad ʿAndalīb), the *Nāla-i ʿAndalīb* (The Lament of the Nightingale), the mystical union between God and the soul is described unequivocally as the consummation of marriage in which the bride becomes aware of the powerful *jalālī* (majestic side) of the divine beloved who pierces her body. In this case, however, we are dealing with the longing for union with God, not with the Prophet. ʿAbd ur-Raʾūf Bhaṭṭī and his followers certainly did not go that far, but the theme of the mystical marriage and the Prophet as the ideal spiritual bridegroom looms large in Sindhi poetry. To interpret this symbolism at a deeper, more esoteric, level may be reading too much into the verses of a poet writing for the predominantly rural people of the lower Indus valley.

The texts offered in this volume prove that love of the Prophet was, and still is, a deeply rooted feeling in all corners of the Islamic world. While devoted Muslim poets have described Muḥammad's radiance as a reflection of divine majesty and beauty, they have also portrayed him as a human being, as someone whom the faithful could truly love and trust, and as one who was worthy of the most beautiful epithets. It would have been easy to add other verses in honor of the Prophet—the loving and tender descriptions of his miraculous birth or the tales of his heavenly journey, which adorn great Persian, Urdu, and Turkish epics. These stories have inspired folk poets in all regions of the Muslim world from the Middle Ages onward. Such verses shaped the picture of the Prophet in the believers' minds and they, in turn, expressed their love for him in images from their own traditions—in words that were born from their own loving experiences and that came straight from their hearts. Based on deeply felt emotions, their depictions of the Prophet seem sometimes to contradict conventional theological and doctrinal attitudes.

Poetry of this kind allows us a glimpse into the very soul of Muslim piety. It enables us to define the importance of the Prophet's role for the believers more distinctly and to understand and appreciate his central role, which is so often overlooked by non-Muslims. As Muḥammad Iqbāl (d. 1938) wrote of the Muslim community and the Prophet in his Persian poem *Asrār-i Khūdī* (The Secrets of the Self):

> We are like a rose with a hundred petals but one fragrance;
> He is the soul, and he is one.

It is this very fragrance that exudes from the poems we have examined here—be they from Egypt or the Indian subcontinent. These poems convey to us some idea of the Prophet's very significant position in the hearts of his followers.

APPENDIX 1

Selection of Poetry in Praise of the Prophet

Translations of Sindhi *maulūds* by ʿAbd ur-Raʾūf Bhaṭṭī (d. 1752).[1]

Refrain: My moist [tearful] eyes remember the lord [Muḥammad]
The sweetest of relationships is that with the Prophet; all the rest are meaningless!
The Creator created you [Muḥammad] in the highest rank.
My moist eyes. . . .
The Lady Āmina gave birth to the lord smilingly.
My moist eyes. . . .
O Muḥammad, the Arab, I, "the sinner," am afraid
My moist eyes. . . . (1)

Refrain: The chief of princes was born; the prince of apostles has come!
The lord [Muḥammad] is my beloved, adorn him with wondrous colour.

---

1. Numbers in parentheses refer to the poem number of the original Sindhi text in Nabibakhsh Baloch, ed., *Maulūd* (Hyderabad, Sind: Sindhi Adabi Board, 1961), 5–33.

Gently rub my beloved with *cūhā,*[2] sandalwood and *kevṛā*[3]
Around the neck of that dear Punhuṅ[4] place a necklace of diamonds.
Lord, fulfill all the hopes of ʿAbd ur-Raʾūf. (2)

Refrain: Long may he live, the bridegroom, Muḥammad the Arab; seek mercy from him who is filled with mercy.
Beauteous guidance came into existence when the prince Prophet was born
As the chief of the lords grew up the world was fragrant with perfumes and ambergris.
This grieved one has come to your door; hearing his grievances, console him!
The "sinner" ʿAbd ur-Raʾūf has come to you [O Prophet] accept his pleas. (3)

Refrain: I will marry you [Muḥammad] to a rich princess.
I will spend my entire life as your slave;
Goods, wealth and household items, the Lord will provide as dowry.
For the bridegroom Prophet I will sacrifice ten million rubies.
All ornaments will be of gold, and clothes embroidered with silver.
The "sinner" ʿAbd ur-Raʾūf says, "I have met the beloved, the consoler!" (7)

Refrain: Welcome to that bridegroom Muḥammad, the Hāshimī[5]
He comes! the master for whom the fragrant bed has been spread
He comes with ten million angels as his attendants!
Prince Aḥmad's[6] attendants have seated their hero in their midst
The beloved came and strolled around ʿAbd ur-Raʾūf's courtyard. (9)

Refrain: Weddings! what enjoyment, what fun!
On the Prophet's wedding night, the *ḥūr*[7] make joyful noises
The parrots in the meadows, the nightingales in the gardens;
The bridegroom mounted the horse, [seated] on a gold saddlecloth.
The lord sat on the bed; roses strewn on the cushions!
Come Muḥammad, come and meet the "sinner" ʿAbd ur-Raʾūf. (10)

Refrain: O bridegroom support of the world; O handsome leader
The lord tied on you the turban of honor, the turban of faith.

---

2. Perfumed oil.
3. Fragrance from a sweet-smelling plant.
4. Hero of a popular Sindhi romance; used in Bhaṭṭī's poetry as a poetic symbol for the Prophet.
5. A reference to the Prophet's Arabian clan, the Banu Hāshim.
6. Aḥmad, an alternate name for the Prophet.
7. Paradisical virgins.

On the Prophet's wedding night, the *ḥūr* tied garlands
On the Prophet's henna night, ten million angels are present
The "sinner" ʿAbd ur-Raʾūf says, "Grant us good fortune, master." (16)

Refrain: Muḥammad, you went on the *miʿrāj*[8]; the angels said: "Welcome!"
The inhabitants of the heavens said: "Welcome, a hundred welcomes!"
[The angel] Gabriel aroused him [Muḥammad] from his pure sleep;
The Lord sent for him: "Let's go, beloved of the Lord."
Accompanying the Prophet's mount were angels in close proximity.
How many thousands there were, standing respectfully!
The *ḥūr* adorned themselves with garlands, on account of the master;
"You are most welcome, virtuous beloved; sweetheart, the heart longs for you!"
There is no one indigent and sinful like me [the poet]
ʿAbd ur-Raʾūf will be saved, along with the *umma*,[9] in the next world. (18)

Refrain: Remembering, my little heart longs for the beloved [Puṅhuṅ]
Difficult desolate distances, dear Puṅhuṅ makes me travel.
Remembering, my little heart longs for the beloved.
O Generous One, show me the tomb of the Prophet!
Remembering, my little heart longs for the beloved.
Woe on my condition that I forgot his abode!
Remembering, my little heart longs for the beloved.
Love for Medina kills the "sinner" ʿAbd ur-Raʾūf.
Remembering, my little heart longs for the beloved. (45)

Refrain: O love-intoxicated Muḥammad, meet your yearning lovers.
Countless beings have sacrificed themselves, Muḥammad, meet your yearning lovers.
For the youthful beloved, the Sassuis[10] have been pining
O love-intoxicated Muḥammad . . .
When it [love] took firm hold, I listened to no one and nothing!
O love-intoxicated Muḥammad . . .
Those who leave their homeland, they smile in the middle of the battle-field[11]
O love-intoxicated Muḥammad . . .

---

8. The Prophet's ascension and mystical journey to heaven.
9. The Muslim community.
10. Sassui, the heroine of a famous Sindhi romance, frequently used by Bhaṭṭī and other Sindhi poets as a symbol for the woman-soul.
11. An allusion to the painful struggles experienced by the woman-soul in quest for its beloved.

The moths of the beloved Prophet burn while they circle
O love-intoxicated Muḥammad . . .
I, the slaughtered lover, sacrifice myself for Prince Aḥmad
O love-intoxicated Muḥammad . . .
The lover, ʿAbd ur-Raʾūf says, "Honor is appropriate to [his] status"
O love-intoxicated Muḥammad . . . (48)

Refrain: No sickness afflicts me; I am afflicted by love for you
I am love-sick: beloved you be my health!
The beloved need only come to my house and all pains and afflictions will be cured.
If he [the beloved] curtails the pain, the soul gets peace;
My master, come to me, come to me! an end to this separation!
O sweetheart, if I were to meet you, then so quickly would all afflictions depart!
O Meccan sir, as dowry, cover [i.e., put a lid on] the vessel of pains
Kissing you on the head, I say, I will be entrusted to you
The "sinner" ʿAbd ur-Raʾūf says, "Grant me a place in paradise." (49)

Refrain: I pass time till the day of resurrection; to whom shall I tell, would that I meet him! O intercessor, O Arab, I still yearn for you
Would that I would give up my life crawling along the road to Medina!
Except for you, guardian, with whom should I talk about my state?
I look with my eyes raised in the direction
The "sinner" ʿAbd ur-Raʾūf says, I prostrate myself before the beloved. (52)

Refrain: Return with news of [our] meeting, why not, O my beloved, return with news of [our] meeting.
The love of the prince Muḥammad in the heart and the refuge of the [Qurʾān] recitation in the body;
O Lord, show me one whose body contains the fire of *biraha!*[12]
May the King Aḥmad come to the courtyard, may the soul that wanders with secrets of love encounter the Lord Muḥammad, may it meet that sweet, comforting beloved!
Deep passion for the beloved entered my heart; immediately there followed pain.
O compassionate one, save me now; remove the burdens of *biraha*

12. Longing in separation.

The darling heart moves toward the beloved, disclosing all its pains to the master;
The dear little soul burns for the beloved, cure this sickness of love.
ʿAbd ur-Raʾūf is a petitioner at your door; Lord do not make him return empty-handed.
You are the ruler of the whole world, o dear one, fulfill your promises. (65)

Refrain: O girlfriends! How can I bear this? I, who am walking towards the beloved Puṅhuṅ[13]
While awake, I weep; while sleeping, I have no peace;
Thoughts of the Hashimite friend overcome me!
Sisters, staying in this Bhambhore is poison to me!
The fist of death grinds me along the road;
Seizing me by the roots, love has carried me away!
The grasped hem[14] no longer remains [in my hand];
I live but my life has gone!
The "sinner" ʿAbd ur-Raʾūf says, "Treat me kindly:
I am going to the Prince of Medina and I will return." (71)

Translations from Muḥsin Kākorawī's Urdu poem *Madīḥ khair al-mursalīn* (Eulogy for the best of messengers).[15]

Selections from the Exordium *(tashbīb)*

From the direction of Benares went a cloud toward Mathura;
The breeze brings Ganges water on the shoulders of lightning.
The cypress-statured residents of Gokal[16] perform ablutions right [in their] home;
For to go to bathe in the River Jumna is a prolonged hope.
News has just reached the great forest that
The wind-borne clouds are proceeding to the [Hindu] pilgrimage sites.
The dense black clouds extend far into the distance;

---

13. See note 4.
14. A reference to the hem of Puṅhuṅ's garment which Sassui grasped.
15. The original text can be found in Muḥammad Nūr al-Ḥasan, *Kulliyyāt-i naʿt-i Muḥsin Kākorawī* (Lucknow: Uttar Pradesh Academy, 1982), 95–123. The number in brackets indicates the page number in this edition.
16. The name of a tract of land along the River Jumna which served as the residence of Krishna during his youth.

The idols hold sway not only in Hind [India] but indeed the whole world.
The invasion of black clouds proceeds towards the *qibla:*[17]
Perhaps Lāt and Hubal[18] may yet again lay siege to the Kaʿba. (95–96)

. . . .

In the entire day, not even for a couple hours did it [the rain] cease;
For fifteen days there has been a joyful abundance of water
"How will we be blessed with the *darshan*[19] of Lord Krishna?"
The *gopīs*[20] wonder with their hearts pounding restlessly in their constricted bosoms. (96–97)

. . . .

Neither the moon is visible at night nor the sun during the day;
This tumultuous darkness is the influence of Saturn.[21]
The density of the dark clouds is such that it renders the candle invisible,
Even though the moth searches for it with a torch.
The pupil of the eye was concealed in the veil of darkness;
The eye of the world-seeing sun contains symptoms of cataract.
The smoke of the fire of the rose reached the ceiling of the spheres;
Lamp-black congealed on the ceiling of the house of the sun!
So blinding is the darkness that the cloud itself cannot move;
Thunder says to lightning, "Better bring a torch!" (99–100)

Selections from the Panegyric *(madḥ)*

The saplings of anthropomorphism are verdant in the garden of attributelessness
Of which the prophets are the branches and the gnostics are the buds.
The beautiful rose of the Arabian, Medinan, Prophet
Adorns the skirt of eternity and ornaments the turban of pre-eternity.
No one resembles him, equals him, or is like him;
Neither is there anyone who is similar, comparable or who can replace him
He is the moon of the highest zenith, the fruit of the palm-tree of the two worlds;
The pearl of the ocean of Oneness, the lotus of the fountain of multiplicity;
The light of the sun of monotheism, the new moon of the zenith of honor;

---

17. The direction of prayer for Muslims (i.e., the Kaʿba in Mecca).
18. Two pre-Islamic deities who used to be housed in the Kaʿba before the coming of Islam.
19. Literally translated as "vision."
20. The cow-maids of Mathura who are hopelessly in love with Krishna.
21. This planet is often referred to as the Hindu of the spheres.

The flame of the candle of creation, the lamp of the assembly of messengership. (113)

The refuge of the Trusted Spirit (Gabriel), the adorner of the heavenly thrones sublime;
The protector of the firm religion, the abrogator of creeds and nations.
He is the high-ranking King in the seven climes of dominion;
The messenger sent for the four directions of guidance.
I wish to write many befitting hemistiches
If only the pen would not become ecstatic and fly off from my hand!
He was the chosen selection of the manuscript of Oneness on the day of pre-eternity.
There is neither a second to Aḥmad nor a predecessor to the One. (114)

. . . .

How [beautifully] the cloud prostrates toward the Kaʿba, the *qibla*
The cloud prostrates towards Yathrib[22] and Baṯḥā[23]
Having abandoned the tavern of India and the idol house of Braj,
Today the cloud has spread its prayer rug in the Kaʿba.
Having put on blinkers on the grey horse of the heavens,
The black cloud has brought it for the Arabian rider.
In the ocean of contingency, the Arabian messenger is a unique pearl;
The cloud is a special mercy of the Lord Almighty. (118)

The Kaʿba of the eyebrow of the Prophet is the *qibla* for the people of insight,
The black cloud is the hair surrounding the head of the *qibla* [Muḥammad]
Lightning weeps out of envy of the flame of that face,
The cloud has placed a shawl on the face of lightning.
Widespread is the fame of the life-bestowing lips of the Prophet,
Listen a moment to what Jesus says to the cloud:
"Look with the eye of justice at his [the Prophet's] noble teeth,
He is your unique pearl even though you are a unique cloud."
The thread of angels was bound around the holy pearl;
On the night of the *miʿrāj* the cloud was at the exalted divine throne.
In ascending and descending, *Burāq* was equal to lightning
The cloud was the verdant meadow of the world above. (119)

---

22. Pre-Islamic name for the city of Medina.
23. A swampy valley near Medina.

Selections from the Supplication *(duʿā)*

Your rank is the highest and the most excellent;
This is the essence of my detailed faith.
It is my wish that none of my poetry, be it *qiṭʿa*,[24] or *qaṣīda*, or *ghazal*,[25]
Should be devoid of your praise.
In religion and the world I should have no other refuge;
Only on you do I depend, on your strength, on your power.
May [you be] my fibre of hope and palm tree, fresh and green[26]
Whose every branch has flowers, and whose every flower contains a fruit. (121)

My desire is that I continue to think of you till the moment of death,
That I see your form when death comes.
With the name of Muḥammad on the tongue and the secret of "without *mīm*" in the heart,[27]
On my lips be the blessing on the Prophet and in the heart the glorification of God.
May the angel of death, ʿAzrāʾīl, lovingly say to my soul:
"My dear, if you are coming along to Medina then let's go."
At the moment of death let this be the sign of your intercession:
"Don't worry about the day of resurrection, we'll take care of it tomorrow."
The memory of the mirror-like face may confound me,
May I see the mirror palace in the corner of my grave.
May the two scribe angels,[28] my hosts, say: "Feel at home [here];
Don't worry about a thing, don't be anxious!" (122)

May I remember your resplendent face after annihilation *(fanā)*
So that it may come as my companion on the road of non-existence as a (guiding) torch.

---

24. Fragmentary verse.
25. Traditionally, a love-poem.
26. An allusion to the Qurʾānic story of Mary who was supported by the trunk of the palm tree and its fruit as she gave birth to Jesus. *Sūra* 19: 23–26.
27. An allusion to the *ḥadīth qudsī* (divine saying) according to which God declared: *Anā Aḥmad bilā mīm* ("I am Aḥmad [Muḥammad] without the [letter] m.").
28. Reference to Munkar and Nakīr, the two angels who according to Islamic legend are entrusted with the task of recording a person's deeds.

May my sins, heavy and light, be erased,
When my deeds, righteous and noble, come to the scales.

. . . .

May [I] your panegyrist be with you in the ranks of resurrection,
Holding this intoxicating *qaṣīda* and *ghazal*.
When Gabriel signals and says "Yes, begin in the name of God,
'From the direction of Benares went a cloud towards Mathura.' " (123)

Selections from the Egyptian Ballad on the Prophet's Marriage

The translation is based on two versions referred to in the text as recorded by the German orientalist, Enno Littmann, and the Egyptian, Shaykh Ibn Aḥmad. Stanzas 53–57 are not included in Littmann.

The Prophet and the Snake

51.
The guiding chosen one came up and saw the snake
His she-camel was about to be frightened when the snake appeared to it
The chosen one, the lord of the people of ʿAdnān, said to the she-camel:
"Why do you fret when the Lord of the Nation is on top of you?
He is the mediator for creation on the day when the scales are installed [for the final judgment]."

52.
When the snake saw Ṭāhā, the guiding chosen Prophet
It kissed his hands and quietly asked the Prophet for a favour
It talked to the beautiful Prophet with the grace of God, the Guiding One
And it said: "I bear witness that God is the True One
And that you, Prophet, are the Messenger, the guide for the perplexed."

53.
Greetings to you who are the medicine for the wound if it festers on!
You, for whom I have been looking for so long
By the One who made you perfect, a paragon of beauty
O Master, do not be afraid or terrified of me
I am one of the kings of the jinn in a human form.

54.
You who are chosen by the Sole Creator
The One who always bestows His beneficence on you
I have fulfilled my time-old vow

Be my intercessor, O son of Rāma, on the Day of Terror!
The day people will be seen weeping and their sweat streaming forth.

55.
By God, O beautiful Prophet, forgive me, and smile
I had seen God's friend [Abraham] whose words are truthful and explicit
I asked him for intercession for me and he said: "Go to the Prophet."
ʿĪsā [Jesus] said: "Intercession is the doing of the Guiding Prophet
He relieves [people's] distress on the day when souls are resurrected."

56.
Since then I have, O Prophet of God, been waiting
And hoping for this day, O one with kohl-coloured eyes!
O how tormented was I and driven to madness by your love!
And I say, O beloved of mine, "Who can secure us Paradise?"
The Tihāmī [Muḥammad] told him: "The Merciful One will admit you to Paradise
Because with His bounty He is generously merciful.
When the Day of Judgment comes, and its arrival is verified beyond doubt,
Come [to me], O snake, and be punctual;
But [for now] go and leave the route of the caravans."

57.
The snake heard these words and it left people alone.
The Prophet's heart is never oblivious to the mention of God's name
The snake said: "My beloved interceded for me; I am none the worse for anything."
Before the snake left, it knelt down and kissed the Prophet's feet.
The staggering Abū Jahl was bumping against the bodies of men [who were supporting him]
In his heart he had one of many grudges
He exclaimed: "I thought Muḥammad would be bitten by the snake
It turned out that he, at once, enchanted the snake too."
Humiliated in front of his men, Abū Jahl wearily retreated.

The Prophet's Meeting with the Monk Baḥīrā

73.
The Prophet arrived at the monastery; all people rose up for him
For he has come with a religion which the Lord of the Throne has erected.
But Abū Jahl was seated and did not rise up to his feet
Ḥamza, the Prophet's uncle, said to Abū Jahl: "Stand up, scoundrel!
Or I will chop your head off; I will carry out my threat."

74.
At (his) dwelling place, Baḥīrā had prepared for the Prophet
A cushion wrapped in silk, the best of his choice
On it the accursed Abū Jahl, whose dwelling will be Hellfire, was seated.
As the Prophet entered, Baḥīrā said to Abū Jahl: "Get off!
This is the place of the one whose mention illumines my heart [or whose mention sets my heart ablaze]."

75.
Baḥīrā rose to greet the guide; his heart gripped by love,
All distress and agony departed from him.
He went on welcoming Ṭāhā [Muḥammad], the prince of Islam,
And said to him: "Master, you have honored our dwelling!
We had been promised since time long past to witness you."

76.
He laid the tables at once and brought them in;
Over the men of esteem, he favored Ṭāhā's uncles.
He went on welcoming them and tending to their needs.
For the sake of the Tihāmī [the Prophet], joy was at their beck and call.
Baḥīrā said to them: "Today is as joyful as the feast day!
My happiness is total; the hours of joy are [to be deemed] feasts."
They sat at the tables; joy was bountiful
But our Prophet, the Tihāmī, did not eat the food.
Baḥīrā said to Ṭāhā: "O one with kohl-coloured eyes,
You who support the powerless in adversities.
I have witnessed your clear wonders, O beautiful one
What was the reason you left the food and abstained from it?
Tell me the truth, O you whose all deeds are graceful."

77.
The Tihāmī who made manifest the religion of God said:
"The name of the True God has not been mentioned over this food."
Baḥīrā said: "Your words are truthful, O my beloved the true one!
You who have apprehended the hidden meanings while your foes went astray."
He brought the milk for the Prophet who drank from it at once.
He began to thank our Lord for this condition.
With tears streaming down, Baḥīrā said:
"I desire to ask you, O choicest of God's creation,
About forty questions;" the Tihāmī said: "Go on, ask."

78.
Baḥīrā was knowledgeable about the Prophet's mission.
He divulged the secret which had been concealed.

Muḥammad said, as people were looking on,
"I want to ask you just one question"
Baḥīrā said: "Ask, O favorite of God's creation."

79.
Baḥīrā said: "Yes, o goal of what is sought after,
You whose words are more well favored and sought after than any other words."
The Prophet asked him: "What is written on the gate of Paradise?"
Baḥīrā fell silent; what was written was wiped out in front of him!
When he fell silent, the monks said to him:
"Why are you so miserably overwhelmed by the question, Father?
You have asked him forty questions which he had answered and his merit was manifested
Muḥammad asked you just one question!
Out with the answer at once if you love him!"

80.
"Out with the answer at once and say what you have [to say]!
In the presence of the one whose [resplendence] the sun rays cannot match.
We will follow your order and not disobey it."
Baḥīrā said to them: "Say the testimony to the oneness of God.
How shameful it is for one to say what he will not fulfill!"

81.
Listen to me and say the testimony to the oneness of God
It will keep you company at the time of adversity and loneliness."
They said: "God is praiseworthy and glorious
And Aḥmad is the messenger of God and our beloved."
And they profusely extolled the Tihāmī.

82.
For the sake of the Prophet the whole crowd [of monks] embraced Islam.
Baḥīrā said: "Other than the Prophet's religion I will not choose any.
But for him my heart would not have been filled with light [or fire];
I bore witness to his mission even before I set eyes on him;
O how I wish him to plead for me to be spared from
Hellfire on the Day of the Gathering [Last Day]!"

83.
Baḥīrā said while the Prophet's uncles were around:
"Protect your nephew against the unbelievers and keep close watch on him
He is a matchless prophet and all people will go to him.
He has come with intercession and ʿĪsā l-Masīḥ [Jesus the Messiah] had foretold his coming.
Lucky is the one who has spent his money to visit him [during pilgrimage]!"

An Egyptian Popular Ballad on the Prophet's Night Journey and Ascension to Heaven

This ballad describes the *miʿrāj,* an event of great spiritual significance in the Prophet's life. The climax of the Prophet's travels, as he was escorted through the spheres by the angel Gabriel, was a face-to-face meeting with God. This journey, often interpreted metaphorically, provides mystically minded Muslims with a paradigm for the ascent of their own souls to higher spiritual realms. (For a detailed discussion of this religious experience, see Annemarie Schimmel, *And Muhammad Is His Messenger* [Chapel Hill and London: University of North Carolina Press, 1985], 159–75.)

The ballad, which incorporates many folk beliefs and hagiographic elements, was first recorded and published by Urbain Bouriant in his *Chansons populaires arabes en dialecte du Caire d'après les manuscrits d'un chanteur des rues* (Paris: Ernest Leroux, 1893), 79–93. The ballad was later to appear in Muḥammad Qindīl al-Baqlī, *Adab ad-Darāwīsh* (Cairo, 1970), 168–83. The translation is based on al-Baqlī's collection. For a full transcription of the Arabic and the differences between the two versions, see the appendix in Kamal Abdel-Malek, *Muḥammad in the Modern Egyptian Popular Ballad* (Leiden: E. J. Brill, in press).

The reader should note that in the ballad the Prophet is often referred to by his alternate names—Aḥmad and Ṭāhā. The latter derives from the mysterious unconnected letters at the beginning of chapter 23 of the Qurʾān. There has been much speculation about their meaning, but several scholars have claimed that they refer to Muḥammad. Burāq is the name of the heavenly mount which is believed to have transported Muḥammad on this journey.

My praise and greeting upon the one to whom
The pebbles spoke and whom the lizard greeted and said:
"Save me!"; and the seal of the prophets saved it.
And, into the rocks, the sandals of the Chosen One dived.

My praise and greeting upon the one to whom turn
Mounted men for the yearly pilgrimage.
I constantly call down blessings on him
During the long stand and the clamor [of the pilgrims].
When the well-favored one stopped at the cave
The spider wove its cobweb around it.
On Abū Bakr, the Prophet's kin and companion in the cave,
Divine tranquility descended, no doubt.
God had promised to grant them victory.
And that they would be the pain [?] in the hearts of their enemies.

On the night when Gabriel took him on the nocturnal journey
To his Lord, saying to him: "O noblest of the noble ones
The Lord of Heaven blesses you, O Aḥmad,
And He has singled you out for salutation
The governing Lord has invited you into His presence, O beautiful One."
The Prophet was seated and rose up out of joy
Along with Gabriel, the faithful agent of Revelation, he saw Burāq
To her the glorified Ṭāhā turned and said:
"I have put my trust in the living Everlasting One,
Praise is due to You, my Lord, through thick and thin."

Before the Prophet of guidance mounted her back
Wondrous were the things he saw in her.
The Chosen One came near to mount her
To the presence of the Everlasting and Lofty Invisible One.
Burāq rejected Muḥammad and repeatedly shied away from him.
Gabriel said to her: "This is the Prophet of noble lineage
Stand firm, O Burāq, for Aḥmad; do not shy away
Do you not feel ashamed (to do that to) the choicest among the creatures of the Lord of Majesty?"
Burāq said: "Beloved, plead for me [with God] on the Last Day [tomorrow]
O one with graceful and proportionate stature."
The Prophet said: "I grant you protection, O Burāq,
Tomorrow I shall intercede for your safety from the scourging heat of Hellfire."
Her description deludes the mind,
As was reported by the people of the wondrous lore.
She had a face whose features resembled those of a human,
A forehead that outshone the full moon after sunset!
Her sides were the work of the Lord of the Heavens
The Supreme Ruler created them out of precious jewels!
Her legs and hooves were made of pearls;
Created by a Majestic, All-Powerful, Living, Supreme Ruler.

In her wings there were chains of pearls;
Blessed and exalted be the One who formed her!
The range of her sight is measured by five hundred years [of journeying]
A beautiful horse she is; her match has not yet been created.
The son of ʿAbd Allāh, the apple of everyone's eye, mounted it.
Measureless is the merit of his miracles.
About Gabriel, Muḥammad recounted stories
He said: "O Companions, Gabriel has long hair locks

Six in all, each [as long as the journey] of one year
Of one who travels through mountains and sand [desert]."

About the Chosen One you are told stories
Recorded in the biographies by the people of poetry.
That he ascended by night to the Truthful One
On a Burāq that was swifter than the twinkling of an eye
He went from his sacred quarters [?] to the House of God to the Sanctuary to the *maqām* [?]
To the Further Mosque; all this came true.
In Jerusalem Gabriel stood and said: "O Prophet!
Your Exalted Lord and the Lord of lords has commanded
That you, Muḥammad, lead people in prayer."
Thus recorded and said Ibn ʿAbbās when he heard the resounding speech.

Muḥammad prayed and all the prophets prayed
He saw and witnessed; seeing him is the delight of the eye.
After praying, Aḥmad set out to ascend
To the presence of the God who if He says to a thing: "Be!", it becomes.
In Jerusalem the rock said: "I seek refuge from the Hellfire
I am frightened; your heart is full of affection."
The Prophet said: "Do not be afraid on the Last Day
Fear not the judgment of the Day of Reckoning
Tomorrow I will intercede for you and my community
And for everyone who follows the righteous path."

When the best of the Arabs and Persians journeyed by night
A ladder for the Prophet was erected and he ascended on it.
The ladder had one step in silver and the other in gold
And another in chrysolite, thus recorded people of piety.
The Prophet saw an overflowing sea under the firmament of Heaven
It flows from the beginning of Time until the Day of the Gathering.
When the best of the Arabs and the Persians arrived
And slowly came near it, the sea split into two.
As the earthly sea split for the sake of Moses, God's interlocutor
Who made it for safety while the riders of misguidance were submerged.

The son of ʿAbd Allāh went and Gabriel went with him
To the First Heaven at which gate Gabriel knocked
He said: "Open for Aḥmad, the apple of the eye!"
The gate-keeper of Heaven hurried to open the gate
Between the Heaven and the earth an earnest journey

Can take five hundred years for one to arrive there.
Muḥammad entered the Heaven and found its firmament
In the form of smoke; inside it there was a crescent
Between the Heavens [the distance] is as great as
The distance between them and the earth, the mountains and the sand (of the desert).

The inhabitants of the Heavens have no other sustenance
Other than the worship of the Living Everlasting One.
The God who levelled [?] the earth on top of the head of an angel
Who stands on top of a bull which stands on top of a rock which rests on top of a whale
Which is on the surface of the water which rests on the Omnipotence of God; wretched is the unbeliever!
Stand and listen to verses in the eulogy of Aḥmad
God said to him: "Welcome to the one,
the letters of whose name are M and H and M and D."
All the angels of the First Heaven rose up
In obeissance to the one to whom travellers are bound.

They brought the joyful news to Aḥmad, the messenger of guidance
They said to him: "You are the Beloved's favored one.
Among all creation, there is none to match your beauty.
Your figure is like the straight supple bough.
To the highest station the Most Exalted has called you in.
Tomorrow you will plead for sparing your community the punishment of Hellfire.
You will lead them, O Aḥmad, into the right-hand side;
You will take them out of the left-hand side."
The best of God's creation rejoiced when he heard these words
His Lord granted him bliss (even) before he asked.

They moved on, by God's permission, to the Second Heaven.
Faster than the twinkling of the eye and with swifter and more rigorous pace
They saw its star, in it Mercury shone forth.
By the power of the God who has mitigated our adversities
All the angels of the Second Heaven rose up [to Muḥammad]
And said to him: "You are the bringer of good tidings and the warner,
Welcome always to the one
At whose hands the pure water flowed forth
The one who, with his sword, extirpated the worshipers of the cross
And in battling them was supported by his Lord."

The firmament of the Second Heaven was made out of brass.
Its inhabitants ceaselessly praise [God]
They said to Aḥmad: "Most honorable of [God's] creation!
We desire to pray behind you, you be our leader in prayer!
For you are in close proximity to our Lord
And tomorrow you will plead for your community on the Day of the crushing Gathering."
The best of the Arabs and the Persians led them in prayer
After praying, Muḥammad greeted [them] and said:
"Brother Gabriel, lead me." And Gabriel said to him, "Yes,
To your Lord I will lead you, O most honorable of men."

They moved on with God's permission to the Third Heaven;
Their ascension was as fast as the twinkling of the eye.
Gabriel, God's trustee, and the best of mankind,
The Prophet, who is glorified above the multitude of nations.
When Gabriel came to the Third Heaven, he knocked on its gate
He swiftly opened its gate and did not slacken.
Muḥammad entered it and found its thickness
The distance of a journey for long whole five hundred years
Its inhabitants had no sustenance
But the worship of the Creator all night long.

The firmament of the Third Heaven was made of iron;
The firmament of the Fourth Heaven was made of gold.
Muḥammad, the lord of all mankind, entered it
All distress and grief abandoned him.
In it there was a seated angel who had one thousand heads;
In each head there were one thousand wondrous visages;
In every eye there were one thousand onlookers of certitude
Whose tongues praised our Sublime Lord.
The Exalted Lord who is peerless
Matchless and incomparable!

He had a head beneath the divine Throne, O you, who are present!
His feet planted in the depth of the earth's boundaries.
In his hands was a tablet, inscribed on it were the names of God's servants
And all that was created of all mankind.
A long lote tree the Chosen One witnessed
Failure shall be the lot of the one who denies it and calumniates against it.
On his right hand side he had angels for the people of the right side;

On the left hand side he had angels for the people of the left side.
The Prophet said to Gabriel: "O brother Gabriel! I have never seen the like of this angel."

Gabriel said to the Prophet: "This is my brother ʿAzrāʾīl
Move closer to him and greet him.
He will tell you, O Muḥammad, about why they are there."
The best of all prophets moved up [to ʿAzrāʾīl]
ʿAzrāʾīl rose to his feet at once to greet him.
He said: "Welcome to you whom the Exalted One has called in
To be in His presence and to win His nearness."
The Prophet said to him: "I have been called in by the One who raised this Heaven
And flattened the earths and set the mountains firmly in their places.

But I want you, O brother ʿAzrāʾīl,
To tell me about the tree and the tablet.
And the reasons why they are there, and the soul and about your seizing it
And whether the soul dwells on earth or goes up to Heaven."
Said ʿAzrāʾīl: "You who fulfill your promises,
And through whose grace the blind were cured of their blindness.
I will tell you truly about the tree and the tablet
And about their origin, you son of genuine noble men.
Stand and listen to what I will say." The Prophet said to him: "Yes."
"Till the end of my speech, O you who are good-natured."

"Our Lord created the tree; the number of its leaves is
The number of the earth inhabitants, O son of honorable people.
This tablet opposite it has the names of God's servant
In it are registered the people of pious deeds [people of prayers and fasting].
When the life-span of one of Adam's offspring is expired, there drops
From the tree branch a rose; and I would then know his name at once.
If he is pious, I would send for him one [an angel] from those on the right side;
If he is iniquitous, I would send for him one from those on the left side.
These are angels who would snatch his soul by the permission of the Most Exalted.
Life of the inhabitants of the earth is nothing but a passing shadow."

The Sovereign Lord of the nation wept, and Gabriel wept
With the Chosen One, the best of the Arabs and the Persians.
The Prophet said: "O Lord, my people are weak."
The Lord said: "Your community, O Muḥammad, is the best of communities.
On the Day of Reckoning during the Gathering, they will be pleaded for

On the Day of Resurrection, when foot will step on foot."
Aḥmad, the Chosen One, the Prophet of Guidance, rejoiced
When he heard these words from our Lord.
They moved on, with God's permission, to the Fifth Heaven
Its inhabitants were present; their attention engrossed.

The Fifth Heaven is said to have been made of silver; it had an angel
Created from snow and fire; exalted be the One who formed him!
For the snow did not extinguish the fire, nor was it burned by it.
Blessed and exalted be the one who created him!
The angel ceaselessly praised God, asked him for forgiveness and pleaded with Him.
His Lord had given him enough strength to carry on with his supplication.
He said: "My Lord unite the creation
in Your obedience, O Lord of Majesty
Forgive them and remit all their past
Iniquities and grave evildoing."

The Prophet said: "What is the name of this angel?"
Gabriel answered him: "He is called Ḥabīb,
Go closer to him and greet him.
Look with your eyes on his right hand side, you will see."
Ṭāhā came close to him and greeted him.
Beside the angel the Prophet saw the gate of torture and Hellfire.
Hell had seven gates; at each gate
Stood, with Mālik, guards who were towering black giants.
Mālik was seated on a chair of flames
Scowling and frowning with anger as he still is.

When Ṭāhā saw the afflicted people
His tears streamed down, for he is tender-hearted.
He found in the raging flames the young
And the old who were certain of annihilation.
In it he saw women who were crucified by their hair.
Each one had a different kind of torture:
Some people were biting at the stinking flesh of an animal not lawfully slaughtered
But leaving untouched grilled mutton which was being lawfully cooked.
Some people had their tongues hanging down on their chests
With this torment they shall be afflicted till the end of time!

Some people were constantly caught between the fangs of vipers;
Others in hell were drinking pus;

Some people were eating suckling babies;
Others in Hell were in iron-made funnels [?];
Some people were dragged face-down in the raging flames
Severe torture was inflicted on them.
They neither could hear nor see.
In Hell were black scorpions as large as mules;
Its vipers were larger than the trunks of date-trees;
Their venom could pierce hard and solid mountain rocks.

The master of the nation wept; Gabriel said to him:
"Why are you weeping? Everything has a reason.
You see these young men, this youth, and these old men, they were people of [divine] wrath.
These women were the bemoaners who used to slap their faces in grief.
Our Lord has commanded that they be crucified by their hair.
This stinking meat, O beautiful one,
Women and men are biting at—
The adulterers were in love with adultery!
He [God] meted out these punishments on them for this act of adultery."

"Look at the perjurers, O Master,
You will see their tongues hanging down their chests.
The eating of the suckling babies, O Aḥmad, and the drinking of pus
Are the punishments meted out against the wine drinkers.
The adulterers are repeatedly being killed every day.
The people who eat up [unlawfully] the money of the orphans are debauchers.
But for the sake of your grace, God forgives them.
For you are the intercessor, O most exalted among men!
You who preexisted before preexistence at the beginning of Time.
And who are the seal of the honorable prophets!"

By God's will, they moved on to the Sixth Heaven
Their ascension was like the flash of lightning
At the gate of the Sixth Heaven, Gabriel knocked
The gate-keeper said: "Who is knocking on my door?"
Gabriel said: "Open to Aḥmad, the people's beloved;
The prophet who ascended to the seven heavens and traversed them."
Muḥammad entered the Sixth Heaven, found its firmament
Made of precious and matchless jewels.
There was a seated most serene angel
Who was praising the Majestic Lord of the Throne.

While he was kneeling down the angel was saying: "Glorified and holy always,
Blessed and exalted is the One who is Omnipotent,
God the High, the Lofty, the Overlord, the Seer.
He had created this Heaven [as a sign] of His wisdom, wretched is the unbeliever!
He had sent Muḥammad, lord of all mankind,
Out of Muḥammad's light He had created the sun and the moon."
Muḥammad ascended as the angel finished his speech.
He had fragrance which resembled that of musk, O people of perfection!
The angels of the Sixth Heaven were seen
As they were kneeling down right and left around Muḥammad.

When the angel saw Ṭāhā, he rose to his feet for him.
He said to him: "O Muḥammad, our Lord has honoured you
Over all your predecessors and followers
With knowledge and the Qurʾān He has acquainted you
You reached the rank to which [God] had raised you,
A rank no prophet, close or not close to God, had achieved."
The angel said to Muḥammad: "Make your wish and ask [God] for what you desire.
You are the intercessor, most honourable of men!
Tomorrow, on behalf of your community you will plead
With the willing of our High Majestic Master."

With God's will, they moved on to the Seventh Heaven.
They found its firmament made of matchless pearls.
It had more angels than the Sixth Heaven,
And greater and more immense, blessed is His wisdom in the heights!
It had an angel, were he to hold this earth in his hand,
It would look like a mustard seed in a desert!
Another angel who, were God to permit him,
Could swallow up these earths, seas and mountains!
On his chest there was a rooster-like bird which crowed the call for prayer;
The roosters of the earth hear it, no doubt.

They would answer it: "O master!" and with praises of God
They would utter the praises with it and fall silent with its silence.
It was granted the knowledge about the evening times and the morning times;
Because of its excessive ascetic ways, the light of its forehead was shining forth.
When it saw Ṭāhā, it rose up for him
It said, "O Tihāmī, my beloved,

You have been granted the guidance and victory, son of honourable people;
You who, by the grace [of God], have been transferred
From the loins of Adam to Sheth to Idris to Noah to Abraham, God's friend
To the loins of ʿAbd Allāh who rejoiced about you and was rewarded."

It is said that in the Seventh Heaven, O one of perception,
The master of the nation, the most exalted of mankind saw
The house which is called al-Maʿmūr, the one inhabited by the mention of God's name.
In the Seventh Heaven there were heavy rain clouds.
Gabriel stood by the lote tree of the farthest end
And he said: "O intercessor for mankind on the Last Day
Together we have reached my station, O beloved of mine!
I have no choice and no way out [at this point].
But you go forward, O possessor of much knowledge,
To the presence of the Creator who would bestow on you more majesty."

When Ṭ̤āhā saw Gabriel demure
The Prophet said: "O brother Gabriel,
I cannot bear to ascend without a companion; you have left me behind and I am your confidant."
Gabriel said: "O Aḥmad, my Lord has chosen you,
Go forward and you will find the angel Mikāʾīl [Michael]
Who is ceaselessly praising the Lord.
He is standing by a sea, much water has he weighed and measured.
After measuring the water, he sent it to the clouds.
Then, with God's permission, the water will pour on any land."

When the Prophet moved on, he found the angel Mikāʾīl
Ṭ̤āhā greeted him in the most eloquent tongue,
The angel returned the greeting of Aḥmad, the beloved,
And said to him: "Welcome to the one who has arrived in the vicinity of [God's] protection.
The master has called you in His presence, O beautiful one.
He is the God who, if He desires something, He says 'Be' and it becomes!
He asks you to make a wish and request from Him whatever you desire!
You are the intercessor, O most exalted of men,
You who preexisted before preexistence at the beginning of Time.
You are the most well-favored, O most honorable of men."

The guiding Prophet moved on and found Mikāʾīl
Who said to him: "Welcome to Aḥmad whose light is resplendent!

The source of life's joys and the sea of knowledge.
Treasure of the poor and the wealthy.
O savior of the troubled and the help by which success is attained!
O Hashemite, Seal of the prophets!
The Lord of the Heavens has armed you with victory.
You who led the parties [his foes] into captivity on the day of the war.
O Muṣṭafā, without you there would never be pilgrimage rites,
Nor would the singing cameleer chant his resounding songs."

Mikāʾīl prayed that the Chosen One be well received [?]
And said to him: "O messenger of God, you have achieved (your) goal.
Plead for your community, O Prophet, and you will be pleaded for.
For this community, which belongs to you, is the best of mankind.
O how rejoiced they will be in you, O light of the heart!
When you favor them on the Day of Reckoning.
But proceed and you will find Isrāfīl
Seated on a chair and still holding the horn.
He is exceedingly pure, O Aḥmad, and self-poised
None is his match among all angels."

It is said that Isrāfīl is exceedingly pure
And among all angels, there is none who resembles him.
When he saw Ṭāhā, he rose up for him;
Stood beside him at once and welcomed him.
He did not hold in his hand the horn of the Day of Reckoning,
Even though that was the command of his Lord.
Inside the horn were the number of the likeness of mankind
From the first blow, they will be partially [?] resurrected
From the second blow, all of mankind will rise up
To meet a Lord who forgives our sins and evil deeds.

Muḥammad, the master of God's messengers, was still,
On the green Heavenly Vehicle *(rafraf)*, which was moving on with him.
Until he entered into the presence of the One with the lofty station.
A Lord who is most High, Master, and Seer
The Prophet reached the station which no angel, close or not [to God], has ever reached.
In all existence none like Aḥmad has ever been created
From the beginning till the end of Time, O men!
He brought guidance, the divine law, and the clear proofs
His visage outshines the full moon.

When he came near, God said to him: "Welcome,
The best of the most excellent, Aḥmad of the most noble lineage!
Undoubtedly yours is the highest rank; neither Solomon nor Hūd have attained some of your grace.
Make a wish and request what you desire, O Muṣṭafā."
The Prophet said: "My community, be kind to it, O Amicable One!"
God said to him: "Your community, O Aḥmad, is the best of communities.
You are the most favored, O most exalted of men!
Hellfire is for your foe, miserable is his fate!
I have created you, O one with stunning beauty!"

The Holy Lord of mankind addressed the Prophet
And told him: "I have created you before the existence of creation
Before the creation of water and the Heavens
Before the creation of Adam, O Muḥammad, and Hūd.
Have no fear in My Presence,
Honor my carpet, O one of pious ancestors!"
When Aḥmad, the Prophet of Guidance became reassured
The Exalted Everlasting God said out loud:
"On Mount Sinai, I have commanded Moses the Interlocutor
To seek your favour and he attained union [with God]."

When Ṭāhā, the beloved, returned
To Umm Hāni''s house, he lay down peacefully
He rested for a short time, then rose up
To tell his companions in the most eloquent Arabic.
He told them what he had seen is his ascension.
And he said: "My Creator had desired that place for me."
Abū Bakr believed him, so did all the companions.
They said: "Muḥammad was truthful in what he said"
Abū Jahl, the wretched and accursed one, differed
And said: "O Quraysh, can this issue be believed?"

"For if you [indeed] had been taken on a nocturnal journey, O Muḥammad, tell
About Jerusalem, what it was? O one of noble lineage!"
Muḥammad bowed his head, waiting for the fulfillment of the promise of the Master
Who is benevolent and who steers and joins mankind together.
He ordered Gabriel to carry off Jerusalem
On his shoulders and make to the Chosen One, not to deviate.
The Prophet went on telling them about what he was seeing.
He was telling them the truth in the most honest speech.

Some people rejected him, some believed him,
And became some of his genuine and honorable companions.

When the Lord of the Heavens commanded Gabriel
All of the earth and even the mountains bowed down.
By the power of the Omnipotent Lord
The One who rules and disposes and whose actions are powerful.
No stone, no rock, but fell to the ground to kneel to the One who is Everlasting.
The ones who witnessed the proofs
Of the omnipotence of Muḥammad's Lord, and became joyful, O men!
Abū Jahl and a group of Jews were crestfallen and returned in distress and defeat.

Ḥaydar al-Murtaḍā drew his sword
And said: "O people of Quraysh, Muḥammad had indeed gone on his night journey to Heaven!"
He had been taken on this journey during the turbid night;
He had spoken to his Lord in the most eloquent tongue.
His Lord said to him: "Make a wish, you will be granted what is desired.
I have sent you to the throngs of people as a sincere counselor."
His Lord of Majesty has consulted him for what is good [for mankind].
No other prophet has attained this love communion [with God].
Muḥammad is the most favored elect, the one who
pleads [with God] to spare mankind the ever-burning Hellfire."

Our prophet Muḥammad has performed many meritorious deeds,
Some of which include his healing of the sightless eyes;
When he touched the [dead] tree trunk; it turned green and burst into leaf!
From his hands the multitudes quenched their thirst!
Before the creation of the creation Aḥmad was created.
Whoever seeks refuge with the best of mankind will be granted protection.
Among his good deeds was his kindness to the stranger
He was generous with the beggar; he rescued the gazelle.
If he happened to pass through an arid land, it would bring forth vegetation.
By the strength of his resolve, he tore down the foundation of unbelief.

The more I praise the beloved of hearts
And repeat my praise, I feel relieved of weariness!
He is the Prophet in whose palms pebbles spoke.
And because of his awe-inspiring appearance, enemies lay low in scattered bands.
By inspiring fear, the best of the prophets was triumphant.

The unbeliever trembles at the mention of his name.
At the battles of Badr and Ḥunayn, Muḥammad triumphed over the enemies;
With his spearheads he made them drink from the cups of the colocynth-like bitterness.
The Prophet's companions, the people of piety and purity!
On the back of the thorough-bred horses were like the jaws of a lion.

Yāsīn [Muḥammad] outdid the parties on the day of the battle;
The strength of his resolve shook his foes.
He cleft the hearts of his enemies and guarded his sanctuary.
He is the master of the Sabbath; his judiciousness well-attested.
God, the Merciful One, has armed him with clear victory.
His enemies were smitten by iron-clad blows;
Many were the miracles he had performed among the people of Quraysh.
In battle he had subjugated his enemies by the sword.
Every year the pilgrims march in groups towards him;
Ṭāhā is veritably the seal of the prophets!

For his sake the pebbles spoke and the moon split into two halves.
He is the glorified Prophet, Ṭāhā, the bringer of glad tidings, the warner.
At his command trees hurried to him;
His lasting light outshines the radiant lamp.
His Lord made his community triumph over the unbelievers.
He who opposed him lived in hell, O learned one!
None like Aḥmad was created in the universe
From the beginning till the end of Time.
He has come with guidance, the divine law, and the clear signs
His visage outshines the full moon.

I am al-Ghubārī, known among men of letters.
The seeker after my art can never have access to it.
O one of understanding, you have accompanied me on this ascension to Heaven.
Traversing all the reflections about the praise of the Messenger of God,
I remained three months pouring over
The beginning of the first line of verse, adding and saying:
My greetings and prayers for the one to whom
The pebbles spoke and the lizard greeted him and said:
"Save me!"; and the seal of the prophets saved it.
And into the rocks, the sandals of the Chosen One dived.

APPENDIX 2

A Note on Poetic Genres

The forms in which the poems in honor of the Prophet are written correspond to the traditional styles of both Arabo-Persian and vernacular poetry. In the highly literate traditions—such as Arabic, Persian, Ottoman Turkish, and Urdu—one would use the *qaṣīda*. The *qaṣīda* is a long poem in one of the Arabo-Persian quantitative meters and has only one rhyme syllable or rhyming word throughout the entire poem. This rhyme word can be extended into a short phrase or even a whole sentence. Though the rhyming phrase is a rare occurrence in classical Arabic, it is frequent in other languages. One could use the *qaṣīda* to describe nature's beauty or a long and difficult journey. The poem can ultimately turn into a praise song for the Prophet in whom the beauty of the entire universe is manifested. He is both the never-erring leader of the caravan of souls and the goal toward which the wayward wanderer will travel. His greatness and kindness are usually described in highly hyperbolic expressions which are characteristic of the *qaṣīda*.

A shorter form, usually comprising five to twelve couplets with the same scheme of monorhyme, is the *ghazal*—a lyrical form mainly used for love poetry. Often, the reader discovers that the description of the beloved, whose wondrous qualities are elegantly alluded to, is actually the Prophet himself, but one needs long acquaintance with the symbolic language and the rhetorical devices of traditional poetry to discover such a seemingly "secondary" meaning behind the opalizing surface of a love poem.

A poetical form in rhyming couplets (which is peculiar to Persian, Turkish, and Urdu traditions) is the *mathnawī* (or doubled rhyme) which is used in heroic, romantic, and didactic poetry. On account of its flexible rhyme scheme, this form can be extended to thousands of couplets. There are a number of *mathnawī*s in honor of the Prophet (for example, the Turkish *mevlud*, or Birthday Poem, by Suleyman Chelebi), but it is more common that a *mathnawī*—be it heroic, romantic, religious or didactic—begins with a poem describing God's unity and is followed by another in praise of the Prophet's virtues. Often, the *mathnawī* is embellished with captivating, detailed descriptions of the Prophet's heavenly journey. Such introductory poems have often inspired painters to create superbly beautiful illustrations of the "heavenly journey." Sulṭān Muḥammad's sixteenth-century painting of the romantic epic of Nizāmī (now in the British Museum) is probably the finest and most moving representation of the *miʿrāj* as told by the great Persian poet of the late twelfth century. There is even a whole *miʿrāj-nāma* which describes the heavenly journey and was lavishly illustrated in Herat (present-day Afghanistan) shortly before 1500.

Aside from the abundance of *mathnawī*s that speak of the Prophet and his successors (the rightly guided caliphs), one also finds strophic poems in the post-classical tradition of the Islamic world. Poets used to take, for example, a famous eulogy for the Prophet, such as al-Būṣīrī's *Burda*, and split the long *qaṣīda* into lines of two which would then be filled with lines of the poets' own invention. This is how long poems with a sequence of five or six lines came into existence in both the post-medieval Arab world and in India, especially in the Deccan where Arabic was a living literary language.

Many of these poems, especially in the post-classical periods (i.e., twelfth and thirteenth centuries and later), were composed in extremely complicated style with an abundance of rhetorical devices, puns, and cabalistic games. Even comparatively modern works, like the dozens of Arabic *qaṣīda*s by Yūsuf an-Nabhānī (d. 1929), show all the peculiarities of the highest Arabic style, for the Prophet was considered worthy of the choicest poetical genius a writer could muster.

This "genius" writing differs strongly with the folk poetry of the areas of Muslim India, where indigenous forms such as the *dohā* and *sorāṭhā* are employed, and where the loving approach to the Prophet appears even in lullabies and wedding songs. The major collections of Sindhi *maulūd, munājāt, manāqibā,* and *muʿjazā* show how the traditional themes were elaborated in poetic forms which have barely anything to do with the classical birthday poems in Arabic or Turkish traditions. The *maulūd* (birth-poem), for example, is structurally a simple, rustic song with a constantly repeated refrain. This poem's contents include not only the topic of the Prophet's birth but also various aspects of his life and character. To this day, *maulūd*s are popularly recited all over Sind, not only at religious gatherings but also during occasions of general rejoicing as well as at times of mourning. The *munājat, manāqibā,* and *muʿjazā* all employ an almost identical form which is an imitation of the Persian *qaṣīda* with a monorhyme. The difference is that the poets, not yet well-versed in the poetical use of their mother-tongue, lengthen each last word of a line usually by adding a long "a" so as to create a monorhyme effect. Thematically, the contents of these genres vary: in the *munājāt,* supplications and petitions to the Prophet and God predominate; in the *manāqibā,* Muḥammad's character and achievement are extolled by narrating stories from his life; in the *muʿj-azā,* the focus is on recounting the miraculous or supernatural incidents attributed to the Prophet.

Veneration of the Prophet can also be reflected in the genres *bārah-māsā* and *sīḥarfī.* The first is a traditional Indian form which expresses the feelings of a longing young woman in the course of the twelve months of the year. This genre could be used to express the soul's longing for the "bridegroom Muḥammad" whom she hopes to visit in the last month of the lunar year when performing the pilgrimage to Mecca and visiting the Prophet's *Rauẓa* (his "Garden" or mausoleum in Medina). As for the *sīḥarfī,* it is the ancient form of the Golden Alphabet where each verse begins with a different letter and has meaningful allusions. The poet could insert verses about the Prophet into this poetical form. Among Tamil-speaking Muslims, the *pillaittamil,* a type of baby-poem, provided a distinctively Tamil literary genre to express praise and veneration of the Prophet. In this form, the poet affectionately addresses the baby Muḥammad and recounts his extraordinary deeds as he matures.

Finally, one must bear in mind that allusions to the Prophet are likely to occur in almost every poem in which he is praised. Even if a single word of God's address to Muḥammad—*laulāka mā khalaqtu'l aflāka* (if it had not been for you, I would not have created the spheres)—is mentioned, it is enough for the listener, experienced in the traditional expressions, to comprehend immediately the meaning and context in which a phrase should be understood. Many of these traditions and allusions are found in West Africa and extend all the way to Malaysia. Others, like the saying *anā aḥmad bilā mīm* (I am Aḥmad without the letter "m," that is, *aḥad,* [One]) appear only in the Eastern part of the Muslim world. But deeply felt litanies with hundredfold repetitions of the *ṣalawāt sharīfa* (blessings upon the Prophet) and with ever-new repetitions of his blessed name are frequently found in the Arabic-North African tradition.

SELECT BIBLIOGRAPHY

General

Affifi, A. A. "The Story of the Prophet's Ascent *(miʿrāj)* in Sufi Thought and Literature." *Islamic Quarterly* 2 (1955): 23–29.
Andrae, Tor. *Mohammed: The Man and his Faith.* Trans. Th. Menzel. New York: Harper Torchbooks, 1960.
———. *Die Person Muhammeds in Lehre und Glauben seiner Gemeinde.* Stockholm: P. A. Vorstedt og soner, 1918.
Archer, John C. *Mystical Elements in Mohammed.* New Haven: Yale University, 1980.
Caetani, Leone. "The Development of Muhammad's Personality." Trans. R. F. McNeile. *Moslem World* 4 (1914): 353–64.
Gabrieli, Francesco. *Muhammad and the Conquests of Islam.* Trans. Virginia Luling and Rosamund Linell. New York: McGraw-Hill, 1968.
Grunebaum, Gustav E. von. *Muhammadan Festivals.* Leiden: Brill; New York: Schuman, 1958.
Guillaume, Alfred. "Biography of the Prophet in Recent Research," *Islamic Quarterly* 1 (1954): 5–11.
Hamidullah, Muhammad. *Le Prophete de l'Islam.* 2 vols. Paris: Vrin, 1959.
Horovitz, Josef. "Zur Muhammadlegende." *Der Islam* 5 (1914): 41–55. [Translated as "The Growth of the Mohammad Legend." *Moslem World* 10 (1920): 49–58.]
Ibn Isḥāq. *Sīrat Rasūl Allāh.* Trans. A. Guillaume. London: Oxford University Press, 1955.
Jeffrey, Arthur. "The Quest for the Historical Muhammad." *Moslem World* 16 (1926): 327–48.
Kaptein, N. J. G. *Muhammad's Birthday Festival: Early History in the Central Muslim Lands and Development in the Muslim West until the 10th/16th Century.* Leiden: E. J. Brill, 1993.
Knappert, Jan. *Islamic Legends: Histories of the Heroes, Saints and Prophets of Islam.* 2 vols. Leiden: E. J. Brill, 1985.
———. "The Figure of the Prophet Muhammad According to the Popular Literature of the Islamic Peoples." *Swahili* 32 (1961): 24–31.
Koelle, S. W. *Mohammed and Mohammedanism.* London: Rivingtons, 1889.
Lings, Martin. *Muhammad.* London: George Allen & Unwin, and Islamic Text Society, 1983.
Lubis, Muhammad Bukhari. *Qaṣīdahs in Honor of the Prophet.* Bangi, Malaysia: Penerbit Universiti Kebangsaan Malaysia, 1983.
Martin, Richard C. *Approaches to Islam in Religious Studies.* Tucson: University of Arizona Press, 1985.
Al-Nowaihi, Mohamed. "Towards a Re-evaluation of Muhammad: Prophet and Man." *Muslim World* 60 (1970): 300–13.

Padwick, Constance. *Muslim Devotions*. London: SPCK, 1960.
Rodinson, Maxime. "A Critical Survey of Modern Studies on Muhammad." *Studies on Islam*, trans. and ed. Merlin Swartz. Oxford and New York: Oxford University Press, 1981, 23–84.
———. *Mahomet*. Trans. Anne Carter. New York: Pantheon Books, 1971.
Royster, James E. "The Meaning of Muḥammad for Muslims: A Phenomenological Study of Recurrent Images of the Prophet." Ph.D. dissertation, Hartford Seminary, 1970.
Schimmel, Annemarie. *And Muhammad Is His Messenger*. Chapel Hill: University of North Carolina Press, 1985.
———. *As Through a Veil: Mystical Poetry in Islam*. New York: Columbia University Press, 1982.
———. *Mystical Dimensions of Islam*. Chapel Hill: University of North Carolina Press, 1975.
Waardenburg, Jacques. "Official and Popular Religion in Islam." *Social Compass* 25 (1978): 315–41.
——— with P. H. Vrijhof, eds. *Official and Popular Religion: Analysis of a Theme for Religious Studies*. The Hague: Mouton, 1979.
Watt, Montgomery. *Muhammad, Prophet and Statesman*. Oxford: Oxford University Press, 1961.
———. *Muhammad at Medina*. Oxford: Clarendon Press, 1956.
———. *Muhammad at Mecca*. Oxford: Clarendon Press, 1953.
Waugh, Earle H. "Following the Beloved: Muhammad as Model in the Sufi Tradition." *The Biographical Process*, Ed. Frank E. Reynolds and Donald Capps. The Hague and Paris: Mouton, 1976, 63–85.
Widengren, Geo. *Muhammad: The Apostle and His Ascension*. Uppsala: Lundquist, 1955.

South Asia

Asani, Ali S. "The Bridegroom Prophet in Medieval Sindhi Poetry." *Studies in South Asian Devotional Literature: Research Papers, 1989–91*. Ed. F. Mallison and A. Entwistle. New Delhi: Manohar, 1994, 213–25.
———. "Bridal Symbolism in Ismāʿīlī Mystical Literature of Indo-Pakistan." *Mystics of the Book: Themes, Topics, and Typologies*. Ed. R. A. Herrera. New York: Peter Lang, 1993, 389–404.
———. "Sufi Poetry in the Folk Tradition of Indo-Pakistan." *Religion and Literature* 20, 1 (1988): 81–94.
Baloch, Nabibakhsh, ed. *Maulūd*. Hyderabad, Sind: Sindhi Adabi Board, 1961.
———. *Manāqibā*. Hyderabad, Sind: Sindhi Adabi Board, 1960.
———. *Muʿjazā*. Hyderabad, Sind: Sindhi Adabi Board, 1960.
———. *Madāhūṅ ain munājātūṅ*. Karachi: Sindhi Adabi Board, 1959.
Brelvi, Shafiq, ed. *Armaghān-i naʿt*. Karachi: Maktaba-i khatun-i Pakistan. 1975.
Fazl Fatihpūrī, Afzāl H. *Urdū naʿt. Tārīkh-o irtiqāʾ*. Karachi: Dar Publications, 1989.

Friedmann, Yohanan. "Islamic Thought in Relation to the Indian Context." *Purusartha* 9 (1986): 79–91.

Murādābādī, Fānī. *Hindū shuʿarā kā naʿtiyyah kalām*. Lyallpur: Arif Publishing House, 1962.

Nūr al-Ḥasan, Muḥammad. *Kulliyyāt-i naʿt-i Muḥsin Kākorawī*. Lucknow: Uttar Pradesh Urdu Academy, 1982.

Rasheed, Ghulam Dastgir. "The Development of *naʿtia* Poetry in Persian Literature." *Islamic Culture* 39 (1965): 53–69.

Richman, Paula. "Veneration of the Prophet Muhammad in an Islamic *Pillaittamil*." *Journal of the American Oriental Society* 113, no. 1 (1993): 57–74.

Roy, Asim. *The Islamic Syncretistic Tradition in Bengal*. Princeton: Princeton University Press, 1983.

Schimmel, Annemarie. "Reflections on Popular Muslim Poetry." *Contributions to Asian Studies* 17 (1982): 17–26.

———. *Islam in the Indian Subcontinent* (Handbuch der Orientalistik, 4:3). Leiden: E. J. Brill, 1980.

———. "Ghalib's *qaṣīda* in Praise of the Prophet." *Islam: Past Influence and Present Challenge*. Ed. Pierre Cachia and Alford Welch. Edinburgh: Edinburgh University Press, 1979, 188–209.

———. "The Golden Chain of 'Sincere Muhammadans.' " *The Rose and the Rock*. Ed. Bruce B. Lawrence. Durham: Duke University Press, 1979, 104–34.

———. "Der Regen als Symbol in der Religionsgeschichte." *Religion und Religionen. Festschrift fur Gustav Mensching*. Bonn: Rohrscheidt, 1966.

———. "The Veneration of the Prophet Muhammad, as Reflected in Sindhi Poetry." *The Saviour God: Comparative Studies in the Concept of Salvation*, Ed. S. G. F. Brandon. Manchester: Manchester University Press, 1963, 129–43.

———. "The Place of the Prophet of Islam in Iqbal's Thought." *Islamic Studies* 1, no. 4 (1962): 111–30.

Sindhi, Meman ʿAbd al-Majīd. *Sindhī meṅ naʿtīya shāʿirī*. Larkana: Sindhi Adabi Academy, 1980.

Vaudeville, Charlotte. *Bārahmāsā in Indian Literatures*. Ḍelhi: Motilal Banarsidass, 1986.

———. "La conception de l'amour divin dans la Padmāvat de Muhammad Jāyasī, *virah* et *ʿishq*." *Journal Asiatique* 250 (1962): 351–67.

Egypt and the Arab World

Abdel-Malek, Kamal. *A Study of the Vernacular Poetry of Aḥmad Fuʾād Nigm*. Leiden: E. J. Brill, 1990.

Abdel-Nour, Jabbour. *Etude sur la poésie dialectale au Liban*. Beirut: Publications de l'université libanaise, 1957.

Badawi, M. M. "Islam in Modern Egyptian Literature." *Modern Arabic Literature and the West*. London: Ithaca Press, 1985, 44–65.

Bannerth, Ernst. "Lieder agyptischer meddāḥīn." *Weiner Zeitschrift fur die Kunde des Morgenlandes* 56 (1960): 9–20.

Bouriant, Urbain. *Chansons populaires arabes en dialecte du Caire d'après les manuscrits d'un chanteur des rues.* Paris: Ernest Leroux, 1893.

Breteau, C. H. et. al. "Littérature populaire et société." *Annuaire Afrique du Nord* 12 (1973): 265–271.

Cachia, Pierre. *Popular Narrative Ballads of Modern Egypt.* Oxford: Oxford University Press, 1989.

———. "The Prophet's Shirt: Three Versions of an Egyptian Narrative Ballad." *Journal of Semitic Studies* 26, no. 1 (1981): 79–101.

———. "The Career of Mustafa Ibrahim ʿAjaj." *Journal of Maltese Studies* 2 (1977): 110–17.

———. "The Egyptian Mawwāl: Its Ancestry, Its Development, and Its Present Form." *Journal of Arabic Literature* 8 (1977): 77–103.

Canova, Giovanni. "Muḥammad, L'Ebreo et la Gazella, Canto di un maddāḥ Egiziano." *Annali dell'Istituto Orientale di Napoli* 41 (1981): 195–211.

Chejne, Anwar. *The Arabic Language: Its Role in History.* Minneapolis: University of Minnesota, 1969.

Connelly, B. *Arab Folk Epic and Identity.* Berkeley and Los Angeles: University of California Press, 1986.

Fanjul, Serafin. "The Erotic Popular Mawwa:l in Egypt." *Journal of Arabic Literature* 8 (1977): 104–22.

Ferguson, Charles. "Diglossia." *Language and Social Context.* Ed. P. P. Giglioli. Harmondsworth, England: Penguin Books, 1972, 235–44.

Firmat, Gustavo Perez. *Literature and Liminality: Festive Readings in the Hispanic Tradition.* Durham: Duke University Press, 1986.

Jargy, Simon. *La poesie populaire traditionelle chantée au proche-orient arabe.* Paris and La Hague: Mouton, 1970.

Lecerf, Jean. "Littérature dialecte et renaissance arabe moderne." *Bulletin d'Etudes Orientales* 2 (1932): 179–258.

Lings, Martin. "Mystical Poetry." *Abbasid Belles-Lettres.* Eds. Julia Ashtiani et. al. Cambridge: Cambridge University Press, 1990.

Littmann, Enno. *Mohammed Im Volksepos: Ein Neuarabisches Heiligenlied.* Det. Kgl. Danske Videnskabernes Selskab, Historisk-filologiske meddedelser, 32, no. 3. Copenhagen: Ejnar Munksgaard, 1950.

———. *Kairiner Volksleben.* Leipzig: Deutsche Morgenlandische Geselleschaft, 1941.

———. *Neuarabische Volkspoesie.* Berlin: Weidmannsche Buchhandlung, 1902.

Lord, Albert. *The Singer of Tales.* New York: Atheneum, 1965.

McPherson, J. W. *The Moulids of Egypt.* Cairo: M. N. Press, 1941.

Mitchell, T. F. *An Introduction to Egyptian Colloquial Arabic.* London: Oxford University Press, 1956.

Nadeem, S. H. *A Critical Appreciation of Arabic Mystical Poetry.* Lahore: Islamic Book Service, 1979.

Parry, Milman. *The Making of Homeric Verse: The Collected Papers of Milman Parry.* Ed. Adam Parry. Oxford, 1971.

al-Qāʿūd, Ḥilmī. *Muḥammad ṣallā- llāh ʿalayhi wa sallam fī sh-shiʿr al-ḥadīth*. Al-Manṣūra: Dār al-Wafāʾ, 1987.

Shoubi, Elie. "The Influence of the Arabic Language on the Psychology of the Arabs." *Middle East Journal* 5 (1951): 284–302.

Tomiche, Nada. "Le mawwāl egyptien." *Mélanges Marcel Cohen*. Ed. David Cohen. The Hague: Mouton, 1970, 429–38.

———. *Le parler arabe du Caire*. The Hague: Mouton, 1964.

Waugh, Earle H. *The Munshidīn of Egypt: Their World and Their Song*. Columbia: University of South Carolina Press, 1989.

Wilmore, J. Selden. *The Spoken Arabic of Egypt*. 2d. ed. London: David Nutt, 1905.

INDEX OF TERMS

ʿabd Allāh, servant of God, 22
ʿabduhu, his (i.e., God's) slave, 6, 14–15
ahl al-kitāb, people of the Book, 20
anā Aḥmad bilā mīm, "I am Aḥmad without the letter 'm,' " 44n.15, 88n.27, 109
ashrāf, elite, nobility, 25
ʿāṣī, "the sinner," pen name of ʿAbd ur-Rāʾuf Bhaṭṭī, 29
avatāra, descent, divine incarnation, 25
bārahmāsā, Indian song of twelve months, 28, 109
Bhadoṇ, months of rain in the Hindu calendar, 40
bidʿa, innovation, heresy, 8

caumāsā, Indian song of four months, 28

dohā, a couplet with 24 syllables per line, 108
dalāʾil, proofs of Muḥammad's prophethood, 64, 66
darshan, vision, sight (of deity), 40, 86
duʿā, petition, prayer; concluding portion of *qaṣīda,* 38, 43–44, 88–89

ghazal, love-lyric, 38n.6, 43, 88, 89, 107
gopīs, cowmaids, 27, 40, 86

ḥabīb Allāh, God's beloved, 1, 23
ḥadīth, sayings or accounts of the Prophet's deeds and actions, 5, 6, 42, 73
ḥadīth qudsī, divine saying, extra-Quranic saying, 44n.15, 88n.27
ḥaqīqa Muḥammadiyya, "the Muḥammadan reality (i.e., the pre-existent Muḥammad), 7, 79
ḥassan-i waqt, an honorific—"the Ḥassan of his time," allusion to the Prophet's eulogist, Ḥassan ibn Thābit, 38
ḥunūn, songs in honor of pilgrims, 52
ḥūr, paradisiacal virgin, 33, 59, 70, 82, 83

ilḥād lughawī, linguistic heresy, 73
imitatio Muḥammadī, following the Prophet's example in every detail of daily life, 6
al-insān al-kāmil, the perfect man, 7, 13
ʿishq, passionate love, 27

islām, submission (to the will of God), 2

jalāl, (God's) majesty, 12, 79
jamāl, (God's) beauty, 12

kāfī, Sindhi poetic form, 29
kāfir, infidel, 61, 64

lāmiyya, a poem rhyming in the letter "l," 76
laulāka, "If you had not been . . . ," God's address to Muḥammad, 7, 109

maddāḥ (pl. *maddāḥīn*), singer(s) of eulogies, 52, 55n.3, 56, 72
al-madā'iḥ an-nabawiyya, prophetic eulogies, 49
madḥ, panegyric section of the *qaṣīda*, 38, 42, 43, 86
madīḥ, eulogy, 55
manāqibā, Sindhi narrative extolling the Prophet's character and achievements, 108, 109
mathnawī, epic narrative, 78, 107, 108
maulūd (Turkish *mevlūd, mevlūt*), birthday of the Prophet; poetry recited at this occasion and other festivals; poems describing the Prophet's birth, 8, 10–11, 29–30, 77, 81, 107, 108
mawwāl, narrative ballad, 52, 54–55, 70, 75
al-maulid, birthday of the prophet Muḥammad, 52
mevlūd. See *maulūd*
mi'rāj, ladder; the Prophet's heavenly journey, 6, 22, 42, 43, 83, 87, 93, 108
mu'jazā, Sindhi narrative recounting miracles attributed to the Prophet, 108, 109
munājāt, Sindhi narrative containing supplications to the Prophet, 108, 109
muslim/muslima, submitter (to God), 2

nafs ammārā, soul inciting to evil, 78
nafs muṭma'inna, soul at peace, 78
nafsī nafsī, "I myself," exclamation of prophets on the day of judgment, 11
na't, poetry praising the Prophet, 26, 37
nūr Muḥammad(ī), Muḥammad's light, 7, 14, 67

pillaittamil, genre of Tamil poems addressed to a baby, 109

qaṣīda, panegyric poem, traditional to Arabic, 11, 38, 39, 41, 43, 44, 76, 77, 88, 89, 107, 108, 109
qibla, direction toward the Ka'ba, Mecca, 43, 86, 87
qiṭ'a, fragmentary verse, 88

rabāba, "spike-fiddle, rebec, 54
rafraf, heavenly vehicle, 103

sabk-i hindī, Indian style of Persian poetry, 42, 43, 76
salām, peace, 2
ṣalāwāt, formula of blessing upon the prophet Muḥammad, 6, 109
  as way of expressing devotion to the Prophet, 1, 23
  recitation by bees creates sweetness in honey, 13

recitation creates sweetness in human hearts, 13
sayyids, descendants of prophet Muḥammad, 13, 37
shafīʿ, intercessor, 22
shahāda, Islamic profession of faith, 2, 5, 26, 73
shamāʾil, noble qualities and physical attributes of the Prophet, 64, 65, 66, 67
shirk, associating partners with God, 8
sīḥarfī, lit. "30 letters"; poem with each verse beginning with a different letter of the alphabet, 109
sorāṭhā, a couplet with 24 syllables per line, 108
suhāg, state of marital bliss, 36
sunna, custom or way of the Prophet, 2, 5

ṭarīqa Muḥammadiyya, the Muhammadan path, 26
tashbīb, exordium of the *qaṣīda*, 38, 40, 41, 43, 85
taʿṭīrat maulid, semi-rhymed prose passages recited during the Prophet's birthday, 52
thal, refrain in Sindhi *maulūd*, 29

umma, community, 4
ummatī, ummatī, "my community my community," Muḥammad's exclamation on the day of judgment, 11, 104
ummī, one sent to the *umma*; unlettered, 4
uswa ḥasana, beautiful model (Qurʾān *sūra* 33:21), 8, 22

viraha/biraha, longing in separation, 26, 27, 28, 29, 30, 31, 40, 84
virahinī, yearning young woman, 28, 34, 35
as a literary motif, 26–27, 30–32, 40, 76, 77, 78

waḥy, revelation, 4n.2
wāʾī, Sindhi poetic form, 29, 76

INDEX OF PROPER NAMES

al-ʿAbbās, Muḥammad's uncle, 57, 58, 59
ʿAbbasid Caliphate, 49
ʿAbd ul-Laṭīf, Shāh (d. 1752), 28, 76
ʿAbd ur-Raʾūf Bhaṭṭī (d. 1752), 29–30, 33, 34, 35, 44, 77, 78, 79, 81–85
ʿAbduh, Muḥammad, 49
Abraham (Ibrāhīm), prophet, 90, 102
Abū Bakr (d. 634), 68, 93, 104
Abū Jahl (d. 624), 57, 59, 61, 62, 63, 64, 90, 91, 104, 105
Abū Lahab (d. 624), 57, 71
Abū Nuʿaym al-Iṣfahānī (d. 1037), 65, 66
Abū Ṭālib, Muḥammad's uncle (d. 619), 56
Adab ad-Darāwīsh, 93
Adam, prophet, 3, 7, 98, 102, 104
Adams, Charles, 52
ʿAdnān, 66, 89
Afghanistan, 20, 108
Africa(n)
  East, 3, 19
  North, 109
  West, 14, 109
Aḥmad, as name for Muḥammad, 31, 44n.15, 82, 84, 87, 92, 93, 94, 95, 96, 97, 99, 101, 102, 103, 104, 105, 106, 109
Ajmer, 20
ʿAlī ibn Abī Ṭālib, Muḥammad's son-in-law (d. 661), 37n.1, 65
Āmina, the Prophet's mother (d. ca. 575), 10, 11, 58, 81
Anārkalī, 23n.15
Anatolia, 12
And Muhammad Is His Messenger, 4, 51, 93
ʿAndalīb, Nāṣir Muḥammad (d. 1758), 79
Andrae, Tor, 4, 31, 50
Angel(s), 87, 103
  of death, 44
  of the heaven(s): first, 96
    second, 96
    fifth, 99
    sixth, 100–101
    seventh, 101
  of the left side, 98
  of the right side, 97, 98
  scribe, 44, 88
  at the Prophet's wedding, 33, 82, 83
  See also ʿAzrāʾil, Gabriel, Ḥabīb, Isrāfīl, Michael, Munkar, Nakīr
Arab(s), 19, 24, 26, 31, 51, 59, 66, 73, 76, 82, 108
Arabia (Saudi), 7, 8, 24, 25, 58
Arabic, 12, 38, 40, 42, 49, 51, 75, 76, 77, 104, 107, 108, 109

dialects: Cairene, 54, 72, 73
colloquial, 51, 73, 75
colloquial Egyptian, 9, 50, 54, 71, 72
narrative ballads in, 50, 51, 74, 75
Levantine, 72
literary or classical, 50, 51, 73, 74, 75, 107
Upper Egyptian *(ṣaʿīdī)*, 54, 72, 73
Arabic and Islamic studies, approaches to, 51–52
Archer, W. G., 28
Asia
Central, 20, 45
South, 9, 21, 26, 44
Southeast, 19
Asma bint Shehu, 14
Asrār-i khūdī, 80
Assam, 20
al-ʿAṭawānī, Shaykh, 50n.4
al-Azhar (university), 49
ʿAzrāʾil, angel of death, 88, 98
description of, 97–98

Badr, battle of, 61, 63, 106
Baḥīrā, Christian monk, 57, 61, 67, 74, 90–92
Baghdad, 49, 76
Bānat suʿād, 41, 42
Bangladesh, 7, 19
al-Baqlī, Muḥammad Qindīl, 93
Baṭḥā, 43, 87
al-Bayhaqī, Abū Bakr Aḥmad (d. 1066), 65
Benares, 37, 39, 44, 85, 89
Bengal, 14, 20, 27
Bengali, 25, 26
Bhambhore, 34, 35, 85
Bijapur, 20
Bostra, 10
Bouriant, Urbain, 93
Brahma, Hindu deity, 25
Braj, 41, 43, 87
Buddha, 76
Buddhist, 20
Burāq, Muḥammad's celestial steed, 12, 87, 93, 94
description of, 94
al-Burda, "Mantle Ode," 28, 50, 50n.4, 108
Bursa, 10
al-Būṣīrī, Sharaf ad-Dīn (d. 1296), 50, 108

Cachia, Pierre, 51, 55
Canada, 19
Chansons populaires arabes . . . , 93
Christian(s), 2, 4, 20, 49, 61, 64, 74, 77
Copt(s), 61n.4

Dante, 2
Dard, Khwāja Mīr (d. 1785), 79
Deccan, 20, 108
Delhi, 20, 79
Divine Comedy, 2

Egypt, 12, 49, 50, 54, 58, 66, 72, 80

Fāṭima, daughter of the Prophet (d. 633), 25, 37n.1
Friedmann, Yohanan, 19

Gabriel, angel, 44, 57, 60, 77, 83, 87, 89, 93, 94, 95, 97, 98, 100, 102, 104, 105
description of, 94–95
Ganges River, 39, 40, 85
Ghālib, Mirzā (d. 1869), 28, 76
Ghaṭfān, 59
Ghorids, dynasty, 20
al-Ghubārī, 106
Gokal, 39, 41, 85
Golden Alphabet, 109
Golkonda, 20
Gospels, 4
Gwalior, 20
Gujarat, 20, 25

Ḥabīb, angel of fifth heaven, 99
Ḥamza, Muḥammad's uncle (d. 625), 62, 68, 90
Hanbalī, school of Islamic law, 8
Hārūn ar-Rashīd (d. 809), 54
Ḥassan ibn Thābit (d. ca. 659), 38
Hausa, 14
Herat, 108
Herzov, Zoe, 23n.11
Hindi, 26, 37, 41, 42, 75, 77
Hindu, 20, 25, 39, 40, 41, 77, 85
Hubal, 40, 86
Hūd, prophet, 104
Ḥunayn, battle of, 106

Iblīs, Satan, 13, 59, 60
Ibn Aḥmad, ʿAbd Allāh, 53, 55, 72, 89
Ibn al-ʿArabī (d. 1240), 13, 79
Ibn al-Fāriḍ, ʿUmar (d. 1235), 49
Ibn Khaldūn (d. 1406), 49
Idrīs, prophet, 102
ʿIlm ul-kitāb, 79
India, 12, 19, 20, 43, 45, 49, 86, 87, 108
  Indian, 12, 24, 25, 26, 28, 29, 30, 32, 40, 41, 42, 45, 58, 75, 76, 77, 80
Indian rain songs, 28, 40
Indus valley, 20, 78, 79
Iqbāl, Sir Muḥammad (d. 1938), 14–15, 23, 45, 80
Iran, 12, 45
Iraq, 20, 54
al-ʿIrasī, ʿAbd al-Fattāḥ, Shaykh, 55n.3
Islam
  in Egypt, 49–50
  in South Asia, 19–21, 24–26
  profession of faith in, 2, 5, 89, 92
  prophets in, 3
Ismaili, 27
Isrāfīl, angel, 103

Jain, 27
Jāmī, ʿAbd ur-Raḥmān (d. 1492), 78
Jāvīdnāme, 14
al-Jawāhir il-Baḥīja . . . ,
  comparison with *Sīra*, 60–67
  dialects of, 54, 72–73
  diction of, 71–74
  Ibn Aḥmad text, 53, 54, 59, 72
  linguistic codes in, 73–74
  Littmann text, 52, 54, 58, 72
  orality of, 55–56
  paronomasia in, 70–71
  philosophical notions in, 71–72
  recording of, 55–56
  Ṣūfī influences in, 67, 72
  summary of plot, 56–59
  xenophobia in, 60–61, 74
Jerusalem, 49, 95, 104
Jesus (ʿĪsā), prophet, 3, 4, 5, 8, 11, 43, 43n.14, 61, 63, 64, 78, 87, 88n.26, 90, 92
Jew(s), 2, 4, 20, 61, 63, 64, 71, 105
Joseph (Yūsuf), prophet, 13, 78, 79
Jumna river, 39, 85, 85n.16

Kaʿb ibn Zuhayr (d. after 632), 41
Kaʿba, 15, 39, 43, 86nn.17, 18, 87
Kākorawī, Muḥsin (d. 1905), 37–38, 41, 43, 44, 45, 75, 76, 77
Kani Karaca, 11
Khadīja, the Prophet's first wife (d. 619), 2, 13, 57, 58, 59, 60, 62, 67, 68, 78
Khuwaylid ibn Asad, Khadīja's father, 58, 59, 61, 62
Kīnjhar lake, 36
Konkan, 12
Krishna, Hindu deity, 25, 27, 39, 40, 41, 85n.16, 86, 86n.20

Lāmiyyat al-ʿArab, 76
Lāmiyyat al-ʿAjam, 76
Lāt, 40, 86
Laylā, 40
Littmann, Enno, 52, 53, 54, 55, 73, 89
Lord, Albert, 56

Madīḥ khair al-mursalīn, 37, 38–44, 45, 77, 85–89

exordium *(tashbīb)*, 38–42, 85–86
meter, 38n.7
panegyric *(madḥ)*, 42–43, 86–87
supplication *(duʿā)*, 43–44, 88–89
Madkūr, Khadīja's slave, 71
Mahomet, 2
Mahound, 2
Malabar, 19
al-Maqrīzī (d. 1442), 49
Markaz al-Funūn ash-Shaʿbiyya, 52n.10
Mary, mother of Jesus, 3, 4, 10, 43n.14, 88n.26
Mathura, 37, 39, 41, 44, 85, 86n.20, 89
Mecca, 2, 5, 15, 58, 60, 68, 109
Medina, Yathrib, 13, 24, 31–32, 37, 43, 44, 76, 83, 84, 85, 87, 88, 109
Mevlūd-i sharīf, 10, 11
Michael (Mīkāʾīl), angel, 102–3
Minaī, Amīr (d. 1900), 41
Miʿrāj-nāma, 108
Mohammed im Volksepos, 52
Moses (Mūsā), prophet, 3, 95, 104
Mughal-i Aʿẓam (motion picture), 23n.15
Mughal dynasty, 20
Muḥammad, the prophet (d. 632)
as Arab, 26, 81, 82, 84, 86, 87
as bearer of God's final revelation, 3, 6, 15
as beautiful one, 66, 90, 91, 94
as beloved of God, 1, 6, 10, 23, 83
as beloved of *virahinī*, 27, 30–32, 65, 83, 84, 85
as best of Arabs and Persians, 95, 97, 98
as best of creation/humankind, 9, 66, 81, 91, 94, 96, 97, 102, 103
as bridegroom, 32–33, 36, 45, 76, 77, 78, 79, 82, 109
as bringer of good tidings, 2, 96, 106
as (God's) chosen one 89, 93, 94, 95, 96, 98, 99, 103, 104, 106, *(see also* Muṣṭafā)
as Christ-like, 63, 74
as cloud, 12, 28, 42–43, 76, 87
as column of crystal, 7
as counselor, 105
as cream of God's creation, 66, 81, 91, 94
as cupbearer, 10
as cure, 84, 85
as favorite of God's creation, 92
as (candle) flame, 87
as fragrance, 12, 66, 80, 82
as fruit of palm tree, 86
as (loving) friend, 5, 8, 10, 13, 77
as goal of what is sought, 67, 89, 92
as guardian, 84, 87
as guide/guidance, 5, 8, 15, 68, 89, 90, 91, 94, 99
as Hāshimī, 26, 35, 82, 85, 103
as (good) health, 32, 84
as human being, 4, 11, 22, 68, 79
as illiterate or unlettered *(ummī)*, 4
as intercessor *(shafīʿ)*, 5, 7, 10, 22, 31–32, 44, 56, 58, 84, 88, 89, 90, 92, 94, 101, 102
as Jām Tamāchī, hero of Sindhi romance, 35–36
as king, 87
as (shining) lamp, 3, 87
as lawgiver, 6, 103, 106
as leader of caravan, 15, 107
as leader of prayers, 95, 97
as leader to the truth, 15
as locus of divine names, 13
as lotus, 86
as love-intoxicated, 30, 83–84
as lover, 68
as luminous being, 6, 13, 67, 106
as Meccan, 26, 84
as Medinan, 26, 35, 85, 86
as medicine, 32, 36, 89
as member of the family, 8, 11
as merchant, 57, 68

Muḥammad, the prophet (*continued*)
as mercy for the worlds, 3, 10, 12, 22
as messenger of God, 2–4, 5, 60, 78, 87, 92, 103
as model or paradigm, 5, 8, 11, 21, 77
as moon, 67, 68, 86
as one with perfect qualities, 66
as orphan, 58, 61
as (white) pearl, 7, 14, 86, 87
as perfect man *(al-insān al-kāmil)*, 7, 89
as physician, 32
as prophet-*avatāra*, 25
as Puṅhuṅ, hero of Sindhi romance, 34–35, 78, 82, 83, 85
as rain, 12, 28
as rose, 86
as savior, 103
as seal of prophets, 93, 100, 103, 106
as (God's) slave, 6, 14–15
as transmitter of the Qurʾān, 3
as vessel of divine grace, 4
as warner, 2, 96, 106
as (victorious) warrior, 96, 105–6
as well-groomed one, 66
assimilation to Indian culture, 24–26, 45
attempts on his life by Jew(s), 57, 64, 71
"awe of the Prophet," 32
belief in him defining Islamic identity, 5, 26
blessings upon him, 6, 109
cloud over his head protecting him from the sun, 77
conspiracies of Abū Jahl against him, 57, 62–63, 64
controversies among Muslims about venerating him, 7–8, 14
development of hagiography, 6, 7
devotion to him among non-Arab Muslims, 23–24
did not cast a shadow, 6, 13
distortion of his name as Mahomet, Mahound, 2
dreams of him, 13, 37, 38, 50, 68
God and the angels bless him, 6, 23n.14
God's address to him, *laulāka*, 7, 109
his (noble) ancestry, 66, 104
his beauty, 14, 64, 65–66, 78, 104
his biography *(Sīra)*, 53, 55, 57
his birthday celebration, 8
his custom or way of speaking or behaving, 5
his *dalāʾil* (proofs of prophethood), 64, 66
his hair is "By the night," 14
as dark cloud, 43, 87
his encounter with the snake, King of Jinns, 58, 89–90
his exclamation on the day of judgment, 11
his (kohl-colored) eyes, 65–66, 90, 91
his (radiant/beautiful) face, 66, 67, 88, 103, 106
is "By the morning light," 13–14
his green flag of praise, 7
his (shining) forehead, 67
his intercession for the community, 7, 11, 12, 98, 101, 103, 104
his intercession for the rock at Jerusalem, 95
his (primordial) light, 7, 13, 14, 67, 101, 102
his (life-bestowing) lips, 87
his mantle *(burda)*, 50
his marriage to Khadīja, 9, 13, 52, 53, 55, 56–59, 62, 75, 77, 78
his meeting with Christian monk Baḥīrā, 57, 61, 90–92
his miracles, 7, 12, 60, 63, 64, 74, 105
conveying the Qurʾān, 12
splitting of the moon, 7, 12, 19, 106

pebbles speak/sing his praise, 13, 93, 106
weeping palm trunk, 12
trees hurried to him, 106
trees bow before him, 13
lizard greets him, 93, 106
wolf and lizard attest to his rank, 13
doors and walls greet him, 13
frees trapped gazelle, 13, 105
causes water to gush out, 57
causes date trees to spring up instantly, 57
heals blind, 63, 105
cures al-Būṣīrī's paralysis, 50
cures paralytic, 63
revives dead tree, 105
feeds/quenches thirst of multitude, 63, 105
his names (*see* Aḥmad, Muṣṭafā, Ṭāhā, Tihāmī, Yāsīn)
his night-journey and ascension to heaven, 6, 12, 14, 79, 108
Egyptian ballad describing, 93–106
description of first heaven, 96
description of second heaven, 96–97
description of third heaven, 97
description of fourth heaven, 97–99
description of fifth heaven, 99
description of sixth heaven, 100–101
description of seventh heaven, 101–102
description of hell and its inhabitants, 99–100
meeting with God, 104
his perspiration,
as fragrance, 12, 34, 66
rose grows from, 12
animated world grows from, 14
his praise for the *Bānat Suʿād,* 41, 42
his *shamāʾil* (noble qualities and physical beauty), 64–66
his (extraordinary) strength, 57, 67
his tomb in Medina, 13, 31, 32, 34, 35, 37, 56, 83, 109
his trading journey to Syria, 52, 53, 55, 57, 62
identification with Hindu deities, 25
love for him, 1, 14, 30–36, 45, 67, 68, 83–85, 90
mystical doctrines about him, 6–7, 14
negative conceptions of him in medieval Europe, 2
rain as symbol of his mercy, 27, 28
reports of his words and actions, 5, 6, 42, 73
scholarship about him, 4, 5
speaks in classical or literary Arabic, 71, 73–74
superiority over other prophets, 13, 67, 74, 105
transcends time and space, 60, 62, 74
unites the Muslim community, 15, 21, 45, 80
weeps for his community, 98
Muḥammad ibn al-Qāsim (d. 716), 20
Multan, 20
Munkar, angel, 44, 88n.28
The Munshidīn of Egypt, 51
al-Murtaḍā, Ḥaydar, 105
Muṣṭafā, "the chosen one," epithet for Muḥammad, 29, 30, 103, 104

an-Nabhānī, Yūsuf (d. 1929), 108
Nakīr, angel, 44, 88n.28
Nāla-i ʿAndalīb, 79
Naqshbandiyya, Ṣūfī order, 79
Near East, 20
Nizāmī (d. 1203), 108
Noah (Nūḥ), prophet, 102
Nūrī, Sindhi folk heroine, 35–36

Old Testament, 4, 5
Orissa, 20

Padwick, Constance, 1, 23, 32
Pakistan, 7, 19
Parry, Millman, 56
Pelikan, Jaroslav, 5
Persian, 12, 38, 40, 42, 76, 77, 79, 107
Die Person Muhammeds . . . , 4, 50
Popular Narrative Ballads of Modern Egypt, 51
Psalms, 4
Puṅhuṅ, Sindhi folk hero, 34, 35, 78, 82, 83, 85, 85n.14
Punjab, 27

Qurʾān, 2, 3, 4, 5, 6, 8, 10, 11, 12, 27, 42, 51, 68, 69, 73, 78, 84, 101
Quraysh, 26, 104, 105, 106

Rādhā, consort of Hindu deity Krishna, 27
Raḥmān, Fazlur (d. 1988), 4n.2
Ramadan, month of Islamic calendar, 5
Rumūz-i bekhudī, 45
Rushdie, Salman, 21, 22

Sabians, 20
Saddamapundarika, 76
Saladin (Ṣalāḥ ad-Dīn al-Ayyūbī) (d. 1193), 49
Sanāʾī (d. 1131), 13
Sant, 27
Sassui, Sindhi folk heroine, 34–35, 78, 83n.10, 85n.14
Saraswati, Hindu deity, 25
Satanic Verses, 22
Schimmel, Annemarie, 4, 23, 51, 93
ash-Shāfiʿī, Imām (d. 822), 49
Shakarwatī Farmāḍ (Indian king), 19
Shanfarā, 76
Sheth, prophet, 102
Shīʿī, 27, 78
Ṣidqī, Maḥmūd, 55
Sikh, 27
Sind, 12, 13, 25, 28, 29, 33, 44, 45, 49, 76
Sindhi, 9, 26, 28, 29, 30, 32, 33, 44, 76, 78, 79
Sīrat Rasūl Allāh of Ibn Isḥāq (the *Sīra*), 53, 57, 60, 61, 62, 64, 67, 74
Smith, Wilfred Cantwell, 21
Solomon (Sulaimān), prophet, 104
Song of Solomon, 77
Sulṭān Muḥammad (painter, 16th cent.), 108
Sūr Sārang, 76
Swahili, 3, 77
Ṣūfī, 14, 21, 27, 49, 50, 51, 67, 75, 79
Suleyman, Chelebi (d. 1419), 10, 107
Syria, 10, 55, 57, 60, 62, 63

Ṭāhā, as name for Muḥammad, 89, 91, 93, 94, 99, 101, 102, 103, 104, 106
Tāj Mahal, 20
Tamāchī, Jām (d. 15th cent.), 35
Tamil, 26, 109
Tihāmī, as name for Muḥammad, 90, 91, 92, 101
at-Tirmidhī, Abū ʿĪsā, 65
Torah, 4
Tughrāʾī, 76
Turkey, 11, 13, 14
Turkish, 10, 11, 12, 38, 75, 77, 79, 107, 108
Turko-Persian, culture, 20–21, 45
  dynasties, 20
  invasion of South Asia, 20
at-Tustarī, Sahl (d. 896), 14

Umm Hāniʾ, one of the Prophet's wives, 104
Und Muhammad ist sein Prophet, 4
United Kingdom (Britain), 19, 22
United States, 19
Urdu, 9, 26, 28, 37, 38, 42, 75, 76, 79, 107

Vishnu, Hindu deity, 25
von Grunebaum, Gustav, 51

Waraqa Ibn Nawfal, 59
Waugh, Earle, 51

Yāsīn, as name for Muḥammad, 106
Yathrib. *See* Medina
Yūnus Emre (d. ca. 1321), 24

Zulaykhā, Potiphar's wife, 78, 79

INDEX OF QURANIC REFERENCES

4:80	22n.5
7:57	27n.32
12	78
12:53	78
17:1	6, 12
19:23–26	43n.14, 88n.26
21:107	10, 22n.6, 27n.32
23:1	93
33:21	8, 22n.4
33:56	23n.14
41:6	4n.3
53	6, 12
54:1	7, 12, 19
89:27	78
92	14
93	13
112	2